Table of Contents

Introduction
- Disclaimer/Copyright
- Flexi Lexi Fitness
- About Me Basics
- Myths About Handstands
- Why Handstand?
- Keys to Successful Inversions

Warm Up Essentials - 15
- Wrists/Forearms
- Shoulders/Back
- Side Body

Full Body Strengtheners - 34

The Art of Falling - 45

Alignment Breakdown - 50
- Hand Positioning
- Arms/Shoulders
- Gaze
- Back/Core/G
- Legs/Feet

Wall-Assisted Drills - 72

Free-Standing Drills - 81

Partner Drills - 85

Restorative Poses - 94

Flows - 103
- Mini Flow
- Full Length Flow

Closing - 109
- One Final Word
- Acknowledgements
- Sneak Peek: The Beginner's Guide to Handstand Pressing

Disclaimers

The content of **The Beginner's Guide to Handstand**, including text, graphics, and images, are for informational purposes only. Always consult your physician or other qualified health provider with any questions you may have regarding a medical condition, or before starting any exercise program.

Any involvement in yoga or fitness training, including that described in **The Beginner's Guide to Handstand**, can be strenuous and carries a significant risk of damage to property, personal injury, illness, or even death. You participate at your own risk. **The Beginner's Guide to Handstand**, Stephanie Góngora, and/or Casa Colibri assume no responsibility for any and all of the risks described above that may be sustained through the use of this product and the advice herein.

The advice given through **The Beginner's Guide to Handstand** is in no way intended to be a substitute for professional medical advice and/or personalized yoga and fitness guidance. Discontinue any exercise that causes you pain, severe discomfort, nausea, dizziness, or shortness of breath and consult a medical expert.

Start slowly and at the level that is appropriate for you. Not all exercise plans are suitable for everyone.

Copyright & Usage

Copyright

© Stephanie Góngora and **The Beginner's Guide to Handstand**, 2016. All rights are reserved for the content of **The Beginner's Guide to Handstand**. Unauthorized use and/or duplication of this material without express and written permission from this book's author and/or owner is strictly prohibited. Excerpts and links may be used, provided that full and clear credit is given to Stephanie Góngora and **The Beginner's Guide to Handstand** with appropriate and specific direction to the original content.

Usage

All of the information, exercises, and drills in this book are meant as guided suggestions, based off of personal practice and experience. Everyone's body is different, so please modify as needed and always do what is best for your body long-term.

It is highly recommended that certain warm ups, including the ones described herein, always be included before jumping into the wall-based or free-standing handstand drills. Start slowly, and take notice of how you feel after each practice session.

Designed and Photographed by Rabah Rahil - http://sqcr.co

FLEXI LEXI FITNESS

A big thank you to Flexi Lexi Fitness (@flexilexi_fitness) for sponsoring this E-Book and providing all of the beautiful and colorful yoga gear featured on these pages.

Flexi Lexi is based in Thailand, and has one of the widest varieties of leggings, bralettes, loose pants, bikinis, malas, and shorts available. Personally, I am a huge fan of their strappy tops (you probably noticed as it's really all I wear), as well as the cut and quality of the leggings and shorts.

I had the unique pleasure of visiting Micky, the hardworking small business woman behind Flexi Lexi, when I visited Thailand in the Fall of 2015. Innovative and obviously a highly attentive and intelligent business owner, I was extremely impressed with her attitude and zest for life.

I'm sure you'll spot me wearing Flexi Lexi whether I'm doing yoga, swimming, aerials, dancing, or just looking for something cute and comfortable to move around town.

While yoga is definitely not about the pants you're wearing or how fancy your bra top is, I'm a heartfelt believer in motivating yourself to get on the mat, and in supporting quality small businesses. If putting on those bright yoga leggings gets you moving and flowing for the day, then I'm all for it. And I love how social media connects us to quality small business owners, like Micky, who are putting out unique and beautiful products with integrity and a personal touch.

Check out Flexi Lexi Fitness on their Instagram handle - @flexilexi_fitness - or directly on their website - www.flexilexi-fitness.com.

As a thank you for purchasing this book @flexilexi_fitness would like to give you a discount on your next order.

Use Code **HANDSTANDLOVE15** for 15% off at checkout

WHY WRITE AN E-BOOK

I've actually had the outline done for this E-book for almost a year. Out of all the questions that I get asked on social media, the most common by far have to do with handstands.

"How long did it take you to balance upside down?"
"How often do you practice handstands?"
"What is the best way to build strength for handstands?"
"How can I learn handstands?"

I would go through periods of answering each and every single question so that no one felt neglected and then realizing that I was spending far too much of my life clicking buttons on my tiny device instead of getting out there and doing my yoga.

The thought crossed my mind at least half a dozen times that there really should be a simple, affordable resource available on handstand warmups, alignment principles, and drills. That way, I could simply refer everyone over to it instead of typing the same or similar things over and over.

But there wasn't anything, at least that I could find. So I began to wonder...could I write an E-Book about handstands? Sure, I had a great deal of information to share, both from my personal practice and the time I've taken to learn from true experts in the field, but...I was fairly new to the yoga world and unsure how my thoughts and advice would be perceived.

And that's what it really boils down to. FEAR. Fear was the only thing keeping me from providing a resource that would obviously be useful to a great deal of people. Fear that I would be judged by more experienced members of the yoga community. Fear that it would be viewed as "selling out." Fear that I might change my mind down the road about the value of a certain exercise or even the validity of a particular alignment cue. After all, putting my principles in a book was certainly more permanent than teaching them in a class or even a workshop series.

But I don't believe that fear is an acceptable excuse in this situation, and I don't believe I should let it stop me from sharing the information that I already do share with many others, just in a more organized and permanent format.

So I hope that you enjoy the following information, and that you find it helpful to your yoga practice. These pages are a compendium of drills, warm ups, and exercises that I have collected over my years of gymnastics, aerials, movement therapy, and yoga. I cannot tell you the exact source of many of them, however, there are others that I have given distinct credit to under the exercise itself.

MY HANDSTAND JOURNEY

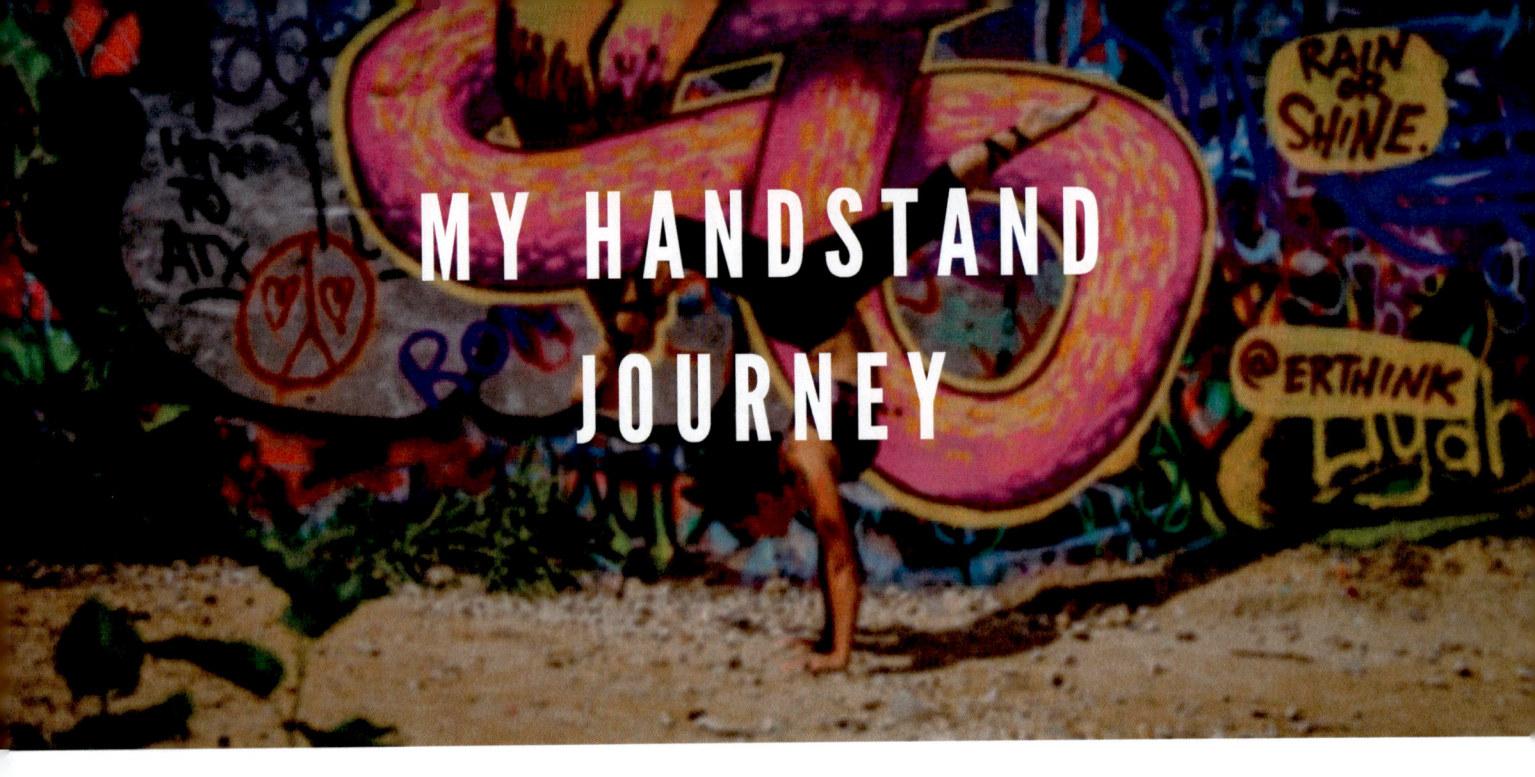

I would be lying if I said that I didn't practice some form of handstands almost my entire life. When I was three, I started a regular gymnastics practice that continued on and off until I went away to college. I never thought twice about going upside down, but I wasn't particularly good at it either. I had to kick up many times in a row to achieve a good handstand, and even then, I could only find 1-2 seconds of balance between walking around on my hands.

So I guess you can say that I wasn't actually good at holding a handstand; I was simply proficient at "falling over in a controlled manner," and therefore, walking around upside down. It was a great party trick, but after gymnastics was no longer in my life, I didn't really think about it much or try to improve upon it until I started a daily yoga practice.

Perhaps the issue was that I didn't consider my handstands part of yoga. Sure I could clown around on my hands to impress people, but what did that have to do with the organized and careful stretching and strengthening of yoga? It wasn't until I stumbled upon Irene Pappas (@fitqueenirene) on the app known as Instagram™, that I really began to explore and realized there were many sides to "yoga" that I wasn't aware of. And that handstands/inversions absolutely had their place in the yoga world.

Not only were people adding inversions to their flows, but there were all of these amazing transitions that came from a controlled handstand. Coupled with the awe-inspiring leg variations that these yogis were effortlessly executing, I was hooked on this whole new world of handstands.

So just over two years ago, I joined what I believe was one of the first #HandstandLove challenges and attempted to not only balance without walking, but also move my legs into all of these beautiful shapes.

I was pretty bad at it. Ask my poor husband Ben about that time, and he will likely tell you tales of me begging him to just take one more picture, as I kicked up for the 600th time to try to get my legs into a pike before falling on my face.

My brain could work with things like split handstands and double stag leg, but anything out of the ordinary, such as tuck, pike, or lotus just seemed impossible.

My body didn't want to bend into scorpion, and my fingers refused to help me balance; they just wanted to take a step forward or backward to correct my alignment. But I kept at it.

After Ben is done telling you about some of my funnier (or perhaps more frustrating) days, I'm sure he would also bring up the fact that he had to drag me out of the studio at night.

We had just finished building our two story garage/practice space, and I spent most evenings doing the very drills in this book to train my body to support its own weight on my hands.

Some of the progress came quickly. I learned to use the weight of my hips and strength in my lower belly to allow my legs to tuck or pike. This was thrilling and only encouraged me to work harder.

Some of the progress didn't feel like progress at all. But I stuck to it, and over the next year and a half, I started to gain much more confidence upside down, find more body awareness than I ever expected, and just experience the joy of learning new things.

These days, I work these drills or similar ones into my daily flows. I don't have long practices just dedicated to inversions, as I like to honor my body (and my wrists), so if I am practicing upside down antics, I typically only do 5-10 minutes worth of my 60-90 minute flow.

But they have stayed with me. I am consistent in my strength building exercises, attentive to my warm ups, and always open to and interested in trying new things safely. I look forward to a joyful inversion practice for the rest of my life.

Steph Góngora

YOUR HANDSTAND JOURNEY

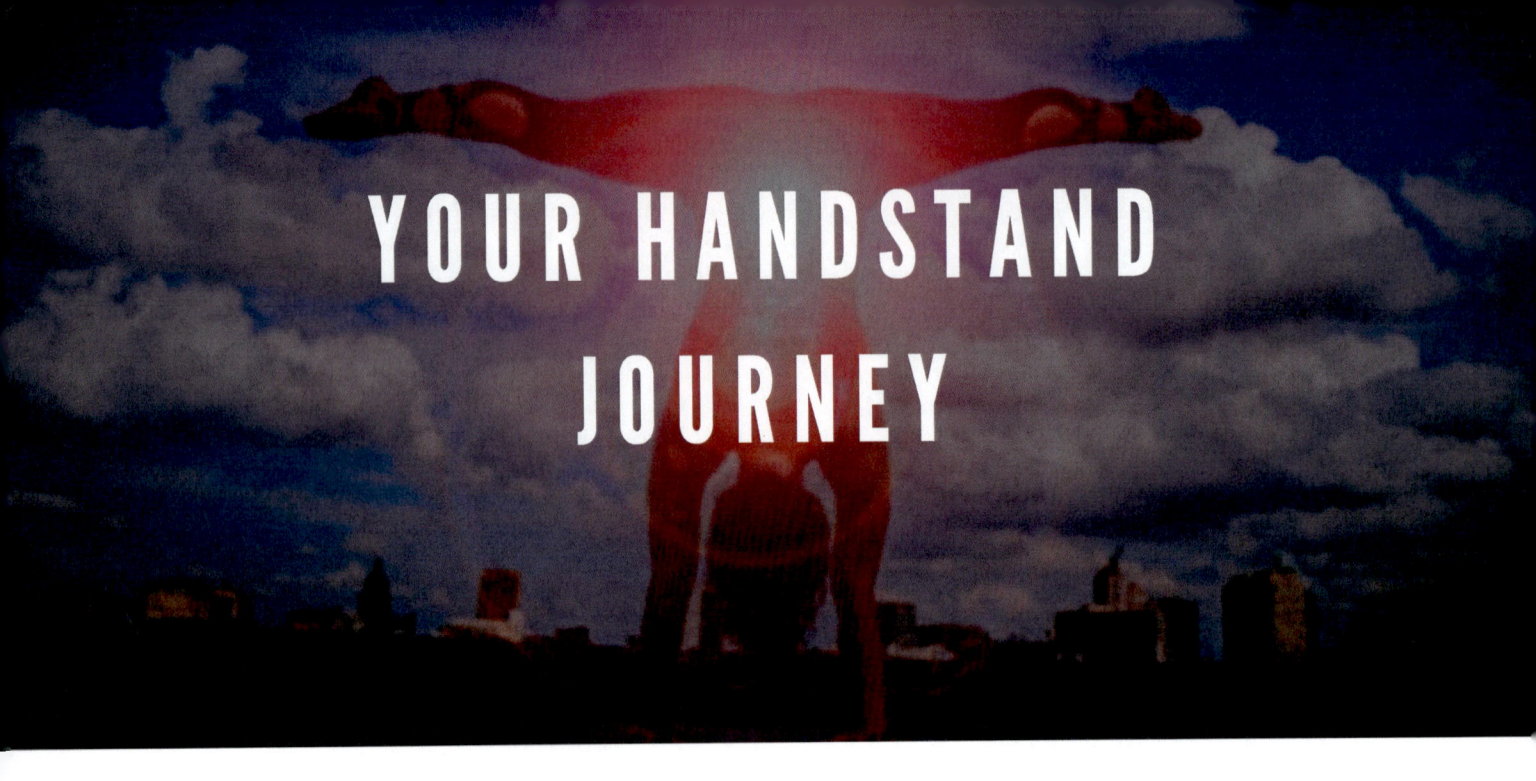

Now that you've read about my journey, please forget about it. Every body is different, and that means that every handstand journey will be different as well. We all start in unique places with our physical fitness, backgrounds, training schedule, and even anatomic assembly. Some people will have "success" with inversions much faster than I did. Some will need to plug away at drills for a substantial amount of time while they build up the strength and muscle memory needed to balance upside down.

> "If you finally get mayurasana (peacock pose) and it's empowering, then that's great. If you never get mayurasana, and you break through self-hatred, then that's much better."
> - Christina Sell

Let me be clear about something. The time that it takes you to handstand does not in any way determine anything about your worth as a yogi or person in general.

And even if you never handstand, in fact, especially if you never achieve handstand, there is still SO much to take from a consistent strengthening practice that may lead to growth in other areas of your yoga or fitness as well. So I encourage you to enter into this journey not with an attitude of "practice and all is coming," but "practice and growth is coming," whether you can see it or not.

MYTHS ABOUT HANDSTANDS

You Have To Be Naturally Good At Balance to Learn to Handstand

I've heard so many people say that they just don't have a natural talent for balancing. Well, neither do I. In fact, on my feet, I'm fairly clumsy and uncoordinated. While it's certainly true that some show an increased propensity for the minute finger adjustments needed in handstand, these are skills that can be learned with practice and consistency. Whether it takes you two weeks or five years, regular short handstand practices can greatly increase the skills needed to balance upside down.

The Easiest Way to Learn Is Just to Kick Up To A Straight Handstand

It seems logical, right? You want to do a handstand, so you kick up and immediately throw your legs together. If you're lucky, you've done this with decent alignment, and your core is nice and tight. Regardless, you've given yourself a lofty goal, and made the position much more challenging than it needs to be. Why? Once you're in a straight handstand, everything is (or should be) stacked. The body is one long line balancing on the hands. Other than some very slight finger movements (which we will get to later), you have no brake, and you have no accelerator.

It is much more efficient and functional to learn to handstand with leg positions that encourage balance, and help control movement. Options such as L Holds, Tucks, and Double Stag Legs (all covered in this book) help provide much more accessible balance for the majority of the population. Only when I had solid 5-10 second holds in alternative leg position shapes did I begin to work on slowly bringing my legs together in a controlled fashion.

If You Use the Wall In Handstand, You Will Not Be Able to Get Rid of It

There seems to be a fear circulating amongst some inversion enthusiasts that once you do handstands using a wall (or with a partner for that matter), you will never be able to leave the wall and practice them free-standing. In my experience, this has not been the case.

The wall not only offers the confidence one needs to get used to being upside down, but it allows you to focus on some finer movements and alignment cues that become body patterns you can take to free-standing space. In this book, we will cover a variety of wall exercises that will help you adapt to inversions, develop strength, and fine tune your own body awareness.

Handstands Are Not Good For You

"If you practice handstands, you will get injured." Luckily, this is something I'm hearing less and less of these days. Yet, there still appears to be a small faction of yoga and fitness practitioners who don't support an inversion practice, or at least one that puts you entirely on your hands. While there are certainly medical and physical limitations that may make handstands off limits for you (please check with your doctor before starting an inversion practice), in general, the body loves inverting!

You're getting increased blood flow to the brain, you're increasing body awareness through small, calculated movements, and you're also experiencing the child-like joy of floating. As long as there are no limiting factors, and you practice handstands safely and with accurate alignment, the benefits are usually boundless.

Learning To Handstand Takes Hours and Hours of Practice Each Day

People ask me all the time if I have to practice handstands for hours on end. Thank goodness the answer is no, as that would take us back to the previous myth regarding the possible detriments of being upside down all the time.

A key to a growing a solid inversion practice is consistency, but this doesn't have to mean consistent hours and hours of handstand work. When I'm trying to progress my inversion practice, I typically do 5 minutes of warm up and maybe 5 minutes of actual inversion drills (which we will cover here). Typically, I just work some drills right into my yoga flows, but don't actually concentrate on the inversions themselves for more than 5 minutes a day. You have 5 minutes, don't you?

Once You Achieve Them, Handstands Will Be Easy

Another comment that I get quite frequently on my social media is..."When did handstands become easy for you?" Sorry. You're not going to like the answer to that one, but handstands are never "easy." There are good days and bad (and some really bad), but in general, handstands still take all of my concentration and a good deal of my effort.

Sure, the probability of me kicking or pressing up and being able to hold it has increased significantly, but no matter how in tune with my body I'm feeling during practice, handstands always take a little extra "umph," and they often surprise me as well. Typically, the first sign that I'm being overconfident and inattentive in my practice is when I "fall out" of an inversion.

WHY HANDSTAND?

Fun

So if learning to handstand is going to take all of this consistent practice, and it's likely never going to feel easy, then why would we do it?

For starters, it's FUN. Yes, it's fun to be upside down, and it's fun to be amazed by what your body can do. Handstanding and inversions in general have helped me see that my body is capable of so much more than I gave it credit for. They have also brought out my inner child and built a sense of community with others interested and involved in an inversion practice. We support, motivate, and assist each other, all the while rejoicing in each other's successes as well.

Transitions, Growth Avenues and More

As if being upside down isn't enough fun, handstands also open up a lot of amazing transitions and growth avenues. Once you learn to confidently stand on your hands, you can add in pressing, lowers to arm balances, a variety of challenging leg positions, and tick tocks back and forth from wheel (Urdhva Dhanurasana). There is always something new to learn.

Throw in additional benefits such as an improved mood (typically related to increased blood flow to the brain), and reduced stress, and handstands can really be a great additional to your practice. Finally, there's obvious core strength that comes from both doing and working on inversions, which can translate to growth in other areas of your practice as well.

Keys to Handstands

01. Consistency

02. Acknowledging Fear

03. Drishti (Gaze)

04. Proper Alignment/Activation

Delving Deeper • Consistency

I can't say enough about consistency. My inversion practice suffers or benefits from only a few days of skipped or consistent practice, respectively. This practice time does not have to be long. In fact, if you're doing a regular practice and warm up, I recommend only reserving 5-10 minutes for inversions.

That's it. Just 5-10 minutes a day. And if you can't get in a full yoga flow that day, simply spend the first 3-4 minutes warming up (exercises provided in this book) and then an extra 3-4 minutes practicing your actual upside down time.

It's something that can be done during commercial breaks, before lunch if you're at work (don't worry; people get used to you getting upside down in the office!), or even while you're waiting for something like water to boil for coffee. I make sure to reserve at least 5 minutes, 5 days a week for some serious upside down time.

Delving Deeper • Acknowledging Fear

I believe that it's completely natural to be afraid of balancing on your hands. After all, it's a lot trickier than standing on your feet, and you WILL fall. There's no doubt about that. Instead of telling people that they shouldn't be afraid of handstands (which usually doesn't do much good), I prefer the approach of acknowledging that fear and then finding safe and more comfortable ways to work around it. I say "more" comfortable ways since learning new things tends to come with a bit of discomfort, at least at the beginning.

One of the biggest reasons that people are afraid of handstands is that they just aren't used to being upside down. Maybe you weren't one of those kids hanging upside down on the monkey bars in grade school. Or maybe you were, and you fell on your head and got six stitches. Either way, unless you have an inversion table or some anti-gravity boots hanging out in your garage, you probably aren't spending a memorable amount of time inverted. Which is too bad because inverting is awesome!

Luckily, there are some easy ways to address this without even introducing actual handstand drills. Simply spend some time upside down or close to it. Maybe that means three-legged dog. Maybe it means hanging backwards off your bed for 30 seconds or so and allowing the blood to rush to your head and realizing that you ARE going to make it through this. Even legs up the wall (viparita karani) can help you practice the initial experience of what it feels like to flip your perspective. Pick whatever is right for you and get used to the idea and action of being inverted. Note: If you're not used to a regular inversion practice, make sure to sit up slowly after inverting to let your body acclimate. Start with shorter intervals and increase with practice.

The other major fear associated with handstands is the fear of falling. As I said earlier, this is legitimate. You will fall. Many times. It's best to acknowledge that and focus on learning to fall safely. This book will give you some key pointers on the suggested methods to fall safely so that after a few dozen pirouette/cartwheel falls (described later), you won't think twice about it. When I first started my inversion practice and was focusing on kicking up and holding a balanced handstand without walking, I might do 150 "L Handstand Kick Ups" (described later) and fall out of each one. It becomes routine and less scary the more you do it. If you're doing proper strengthening drills and following safety protocols for botched handstand exits, it is easy to "bail out" in a controlled fashion.

Delving Deeper - Drishti (Gaze)

I've been spending a lot of time at the beach lately (I know, I know....hard life). Beach handstands are hard enough in wet, smooshy sand, but by day 2-3, I'm always excited to try some handstands in the waves or maybe the nearby river. And every time I'm thoroughly shocked at how difficult they are.

The reason behind this is drishti, or gaze. Finding a focal point is absolutely key to a holding a steady handstand. With so many moving parts that you're trying to control, staring at one unmoving spot helps focus the mind and therefore the body. Check out the in-depth alignment section of this book for focal point cues, and while learning to hold a basic handstand, try to avoid practicing them on a moving medium, like water.

Delving Deeper - Proper Alignment & Full Body Activation

Maintaining proper alignment is so key to holding a steady handstand that I've devoted an entire book section to going over it. From fingertips pulling the earth up, to a solid core, activated glutes, and fierce toes, the entire body is involved in controlling the balance needed to get and stay upside down.

While it may be impossible to think about every cue for every body part while upside down, practicing them in some of the warm up and strengthening postures/drills can help cement patterns in our bodies and make it easier to repeat them later on, even when the world is literally flipped on its head.

Warm Up Essentials

Let's get to moving! But before you're getting into some serious inversion drills, it is absolutely essential to warm up key areas of the body. This section will share various stretching and strengthening exercises to help progress your practice and keep your body safe while doing it.

Recommended (but not necessary) props include 2 yoga blocks and a strap. Please note that you can create your own yoga blocks using books or boxes and that scarves typically make excellent straps.

Wrists & Forearms

Handstands ask a lot of our wrists, proper alignment or not. They are smaller and more mobile than our ankles, which makes them more susceptible to injury. If you're going to be practicing a fair share of handstands, or even other wrist weight-bearing postures such as downward facing dog, plank, and Chaturanga Dandasana, giving yourself time for a proper wrist warm up will help prevent injury and keep your body healthy for a long life of inversions and handstand play.

And these warm ups do not have to be just at the beginning of your practice. I tend to sprinkle them throughout, always warming up and lubricating my joints before inversions, between them, and at the end to provide relief to tired wrists.

I'm typically the yogi who follows exactly what the teacher says to do in a public class, but I refuse to shirk on my wrist warm ups, and will stop and do my own drills if I feel my body isn't properly warmed up and ready for the asana that is suggested. Who knows, maybe the teacher will even ask you what you're doing and why you're doing it, and you'll plant a seed for some of their next flows. Regardless, never neglect your wrists!

Shake Outs + Rolls

Sitting in hero, easy sit, or with sit bones on heels, shake the wrists vigorously up and down, back and forth, and around in a circle.

Suggestion: 3 sets of 15-20 seconds.

Clasp hands in front of you, intertwining fingers and pressing palms together. Keeping palms together, roll clockwise and then counterclockwise.

Suggestion: Clockwise for 10 seconds and counterclockwise for 10 seconds with alternative grip.

Table Top Stretches

Start in a table top position with shoulders over wrists, hips over knees.
Slowly turn hands around, over, to the side, backwards, on their backs, etc.
If comfortable, you can also rock slowly side to side or front to back.

Suggestion: Hold 3-5 seconds per position

Palm Roll Ups

(1) Start in a modified table top position with shoulders leaning slightly over wrists, hands are shoulder width apart and parallel or slightly turned out.

(2) Making sure to do both hands at exactly the same time, inhale and peel both palms off the ground so that only the fingers remain planted.

(3) Exhale to lower both palms in a controlled fashion at exactly the same time

1

2

3

Suggestion: Repeat 2 sets of 15

Palm Roll Ups (2)

If this becomes simple, you can back up your knees for a longer table top, or even go all the way to plank, but make sure that the shoulders always stay slightly over the wrists and that both palms lift and descend together.

Note: These can also be done faster than one per every other breath. Just make sure to move with control.

Drill learned from Carson Clay Calhoun Inversion Workshops

Suggestion: Repeat 2 sets of 15

Fist Push Ups

(1) Start in a modified table top with shoulders leaning slightly over wrists, hands balled up into fists (shoulder distance apart), inner hand (index finger and thumb) facing the front of the mat. First metacarpal (finger joint) supports the body.

(2-3) Exhale and bend the elbows out to the sides to lower the chest towards the earth, moving the hands from the first finger joint to the back of the hands. As with previous drill, both hands must transition together.

(4) Inhale to straighten your arms and "pop" both hands back into fists, resting once again on the first finger metacarpal, thumb and inside edge of index finger facing forward.

1

2

3

4

Suggestion: Repeat 2 sets of 15

Fist Push Ups (2)

If this becomes simple, you can back up your knees for a longer table top, or even go all the way to plank, but make sure that the shoulders always stay slightly over the wrists and that both hands transition together.

Note: These can also be done faster than one per every other breath. Just make sure to move with control.

Drill learned from Carson Clay Calhoun Inversion Workshops

Suggestion: Repeat 2 sets of 15

Forearm Pump

Start in hero, easy sit, or with sit bones on heels. Arms are up by the ears, palms facing forward, fingers spread wide.

Grow tall through the crown of the head and engage the core, pulling navel to spine.

Squeeze hands into tight firsts and then open wide again, finding activation through all the fingers.

Repeat closed fists to open hands, growing faster as you continue.

Note: Make sure you are opening and closing the hands all the way each time. Forearms may feel a slight burning sensation as they are activated

Drill learned from Patrick Beach Inversion Workshop

Suggestion: 3 sets of 30-60 seconds each, moving as quickly as possible.

Shoulders & Back

Shoulder mobility absolutely comes into play with handstand. If the shoulders are not open enough, many times the body will compensate by creating a slight arch or "banana" back in an effort to secure minimal alignment.

Spending just a few minutes working on opening the shoulders in some flexibility drills and simple postures can make a big difference in proper handstand set up, and even set you up for success with other inversions such as forearm stand and supported headstand.

And since many of us sit hunched over in office chairs or in the car for the better part of the day, finding some bend and activation in the upper back can greatly assist with proper "stacking" as well. I typically place shoulder stretches and upper back work at the beginning of my practice, moving from light stretches to deeper bends.

Note: Straps and blocks are recommended, but not necessary for this section. Books and boxes make fine yoga blocks, and many scarves can double as yoga straps.

Double Block Lay

Lay on your back with one block on each shoulder blade. Many prefer the highest setting here, but it can be done on any level as long as the bottom edge of the block starts at the bottom edge of the shoulder blade. Leave a slight space between each block for your spine.

Legs are straight out in front or bent at the knee, sit bones on the ground as you try to relax into the blocks, allowing the upper and mid back to bend.

Arms are overhead, hands clasped, or grabbing opposite elbows to support head. Weight of the arms allows a light stretch in the shoulders

Note: After relaxing into the stretch, practice activating or muscularizing the areas under the blocks (upper back), and just below the blocks (mid back). This should feel like a tightening and even a slight lift away from the blocks as your chest lifts further toward the sky, creating a deeper bend.

Suggestion: Hold 30 seconds to 1 minute

Double Block Lay (2)

For a deeper stretch, create a loop in the strap that is approximately as wide as your inner shoulder.

Before laying back on the blocks, wiggle the strap down your arms with your head in front so that the strap is below the elbow, moving toward the armpit.

Carefully lay back on the blocks, clasp the hands together and press the back of the head into the strap. The strap supports the head, and pressing the head back deepens the shoulder opening.

Drill learned from continued study with Christina Sell

Suggestion: Hold 30 seconds to 1 minute

Extended Puppy Pose (Anahatasana)

Start in a table top position.

Keeping hips over knees, creep your hands forward (shoulder width apart), as the chest slowly lowers toward the earth.

Core stays active to protect the low back and fingers stretch forward and down into the earth.

Gaze is forward and chin can rest on the ground if comfortable, even pressing slightly back toward the body to activate deep neck flexors.

Instead of just collapsing into the pose, keep the whole body active and try to muscularize the upper and mid back in the same places as the blocks were in the Double Block Stretch. This will help you safely increase the bend and perhaps find a bit more shoulder opening.

If more support is needed, blocks or blankets can be placed under the chest.

Suggestion: 2 x 30 second holds

Cat/Cow (Marjaryasana/Bitilanasa)

Start in table top position.

Inhale to draw the upper back in (think pulling the earth up to plug your upper arms into the shoulder socket), lift the gaze to follow the direction the chest is pointing, and allow the belly to lower toward the ground, keeping the core active.

Focus on squeezing shoulder blades together and down the back to keep space along the neck and muscularize the upper and middle back (in the same place that the blocks were previously). (Cow Pose) **(1)**

Exhale to press the earth away, scoop the navel to the spine and allow the shoulder blades to separate. Head drops down as you think about puffing the upper and middle back up to the sky. (Cat Pose) **(2)**

1

2

Suggestion: Repeat the complete movement 5-10 times, moving with the breath. Feel free to liberate the flow a bit, allowing the hips to move, noting the movement of the scapula as you move back and forth between the postures.

Cobra (Bhujangasana)

Start lying on the stomach, hands planted just outside of shoulders, fingertips facing forward with elbows bent toward the sky.

Press the top of the feet into the floor, activate the legs (knees will likely come off the ground), and gently press the pubic bone into the earth to protect the low back.

Inhale to squeeze the shoulder blades together and down the back toward the sit bones.

Hands push into the earth and isometrically drag backwards while chest moves up and a little bit forward. This is less of a collapse into the back and more of a muscularization of the upper and mid back (where the blocks were in Double Block Lay).

Arms do not have to straighten. Think more about blossoming through the chest than bending at the low back.

Note: Keep gaze pointing in the same direction as your chest. No need to crank the head back.

Low Cobra

High Cobra

Suggestion: Repeat 2 x 3 breaths.

28

Sidebody

I feel a little bit bad for the side body. It gets neglected a bit in many yoga practices in favor of simple flexion and extension of the spine. Doing some basic side body stretches and focusing on lengthening from fingertips to toes can help translate the same patterns to handstand.

Hero's Twist (Virasana Twist)

Start sitting in hero (using a block under the sit bones is fine) or simply sitting on the heels with the legs together and tops of feet pressing into the floor.

Lift the arms up by the ears, pinky fingers spiraled inwards and shoulders depressed away from ears, with shoulder blades pulling gently together and down the back toward the sit bones. **(1)**

Inhale to grow tall and engage the core (pull belly button to spine), and exhale twist to the left, using just the strength of the belly to spiral the body (since hands are above the head). **(2)**

Hold for 1-2 breaths and then release the left hand down to the ground behind the body, right hand comes to rest on the outer edge of the left thigh to help deepen the twist. **(3)**

1 2 3

Suggestion: Hold for 3-4 breaths per side, core stays engaged, and imagine that you are spiraling the lower part of the body down into the earth, while the upper half spirals off into the sky, therefore wringing yourself out right in the center like a towel.

Hero Clocks (Virasana Clocks)

Start sitting in hero (using a block under the sit bones is fine) or simply sitting on the heels with the legs together and tops of feet pressing into the floor.

Lift the arms up by the ears, pink fingers spiraled inwards, and shoulders depressed away from ears, with shoulder blades pulling gently together and down the back toward the sit bones. **(1)**

Inhale to grow tall and engage the core (pull belly button to spine) and exhale twist to the right, using just the strength of the belly to spiral the body (since hands are above the head). **(2)**

Hold for 1-2 breaths and then noting where (2) would be on a standard clock, aim the arms and torso towards (2). **(3)**

This twist will generally cause the left sit bone to lift or lighten, so press down and forward with the palms, especially the left palm to root down through the left sit bone.

Once you have found heaviness and evenness in both sit bones, slowly spider the fingers out further in the direction of (2) to find a deep stretch along the left side.

Suggestion: Hold for 3-4 breaths and switch

Standing Half Moon (Ardha Chandrasana)

Stand with feet together, big toe mounds touching and outer ankles pressing in, legs straight but not hyperextended and core engaged.

If using strap, loop around the back right under the shoulder blades and into each hand.

Inhale to lift arms overhead, pinky fingers spiraled inward, strap stays under shoulder blades (causing a slight lift), and sits on the inner edge of both arms. It should be tight - adjust tautness if needed. **(1)**

Palms come together (still holding strap) and shoulder blades pull slightly apart and down toward the sit bones to create space by the ears.

Inhale tall through the crown, keeping body stacked in one line – ankles, hips, shoulders, crown.

Hold 1-2 breaths and then press hips to the left. Hands stay to together and arms stay straight as the upper body curves to the right and upward, finding a deep stretch along the left side body. **(2)**

If using a strap, lower the right arm to the right thigh. Readjust the strap tautness and use a downward pull of the right hand, coupled with an upward and right pull of the left hand to increase the side body stretch. **(3)**

If no strap is available, use the right hard to grab the left wrist and pull it up and to the right for a similar experience.

(Strap suggested but not necessary for this exercise).

Suggestion: Hold for 3-4 breaths and switch sides, focusing on keeping the body in one plane (think of yourself between two sheets of glass). Often times the right hip/shoulder needs to move forward slightly, while the left hip/shoulder need to move back.

Full Body Strengthening

Handstands are a full body exercise. From the tips of your fingers on the ground, up through the arms, core, and out through the toes, everything is working to help you maintain balance. Which means that we need to warm up and strengthen the full body to improve handstand proficiency.

Breath of Fire (Kapalabhati)

Maintaining an active core is absolutely key to having success in handstand. Kapalabhati (skull shining breath, breath of fire) is an excellent way to wake up the core and is part of my regular yoga practice and even pre/post meditation work.

Start sitting in Virasana or Sukkasana (easy sit) with one hand on the lower belly and another on the sternum.

Inhale deeply through the nostrils.

Exhale forcefully through the nostrils, as if trying to expel something from the nose while drawing the navel in toward your spine. The goal is to very quickly rid much of the air from the lungs with the main mover being the diaphragm.

Allow the lungs to naturally inflate, really with no effort at all, and repeat the sharp exhale.

Perform these sharp exhales quickly (but at your own pace) for 20-30 seconds at a time, stopping between sets to allow your breath to return to normal.

Suggestion: 3-4 sets of 20-30 seconds at a reasonable pace. (Point of reference: I have approx. 34 rapid exhales in 20 seconds)

High Plank (Uttihita Chaturanga Dandasana)

There are many variations of plank. For handstands, I think it's important to maximize the core involvement and use high plank to practice the scapular pushups that help you find lift in handstand. For that reason, I suggest the alignment with the hips being near or level with the shoulders, instead of a traditional straight line from shoulder blades to heels. It is easier to find the scoop of the low belly when the hips are set slightly higher, and there is likely to be less sagging in the core.

Start with hands shoulder distance apart, parallel or slightly turned out near the top of the mat and feet together or hip distance apart near the back of the mat.

Shoulders are stacked over wrists and core is engaged strongly, pulling belly button to spine.

Engage legs firmly, squeezing quads and focus on finding length from the top of the crown to the back of the heels.

Suggestion: Repeat 2 sets of 8-10 breaths.

Scapular Push Ups

Finding proper form in plank, exhale and press the ground away firmly with the hands, trying to lift the chest as far from the floor as possible. You should feel your shoulder blades drag apart (laterally) as the upper/mid back rounds a bit, like cat pose. Keep navel pulled firmly to spine. **(1)**

Inhale as you pull the earth back towards your hands, energetically bringing the arm bones back into the shoulders, causing the shoulder blades to draw together (medially) and down the back, more like cow pose. Core is still engaged. **(2)**

Continue these scapular push ups with the breath, moving slowly and with control, making sure to keep the crown of the head extended so that the shoulders don't end up in the ears.

Suggestion: 2 sets of 10

Downward Facing Dog (Adho Mukkha Svanasana)

Start with hands shoulder distance apart at the front of the mat, parallel or slightly turned out.

Feet are hip distance apart near the back of the mat, parallel, with heels dragging down toward the earth.

Pressing down into the earth through the hands (especially the index and thumb mound, which tend to lift), send the hips up and back toward the back of the room.

Legs do not have to be straight, but should be engaged with inner thighs spiraling out and wide to find broadness across the sit bones.

Think length from the hands up and back to the sit bones as we stretch the side body and pull navel to spine to activate the core. Head is neutral between the arms.

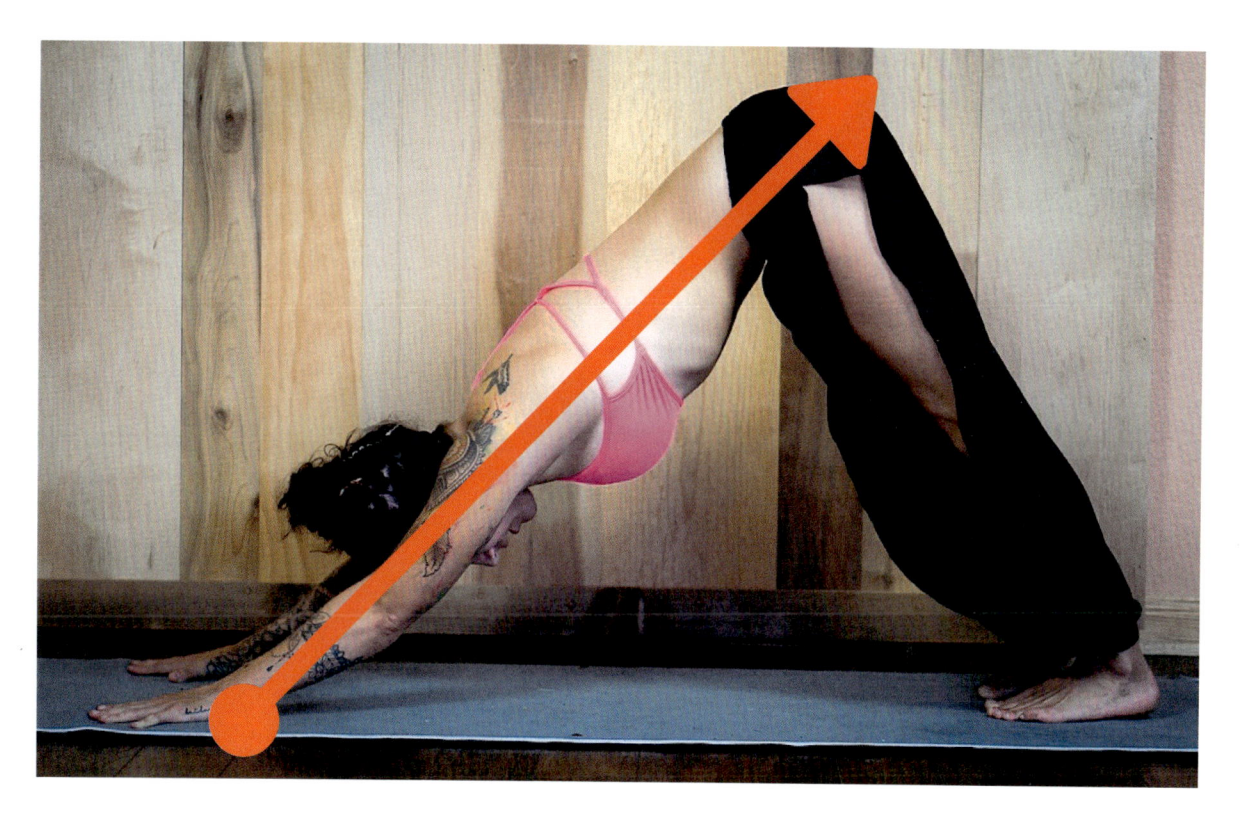

Suggestion: Take 8-10 slow and controlled breaths here

Downward Facing Dog (Adho Mukkha Svanasana) (Tricep Wrap)

To take it a step further, lift the shoulder girdle slightly to give yourself space and externally rotate the upper arm bones to bring the triceps down toward the earth.

Keep that motion and pull the chest down, energetically pulling the arm bones back into the shoulder socket and slightly down the back. You may feel some broadness come to the upper back, while still finding engagement there as well. This tricep wrap is key to stabilizing the shoulder girdle in handstand, but feels much more evident in downward facing dog.

Note: Scapular push ups can also be done in downward facing dog. Simply press down firmly with the hands to energetically lift the shoulder girdle away from the ground and then pull the earth through the hands to lower the shoulders and chest once again toward the ground, plugging the upper arm bones back into the shoulder joint.

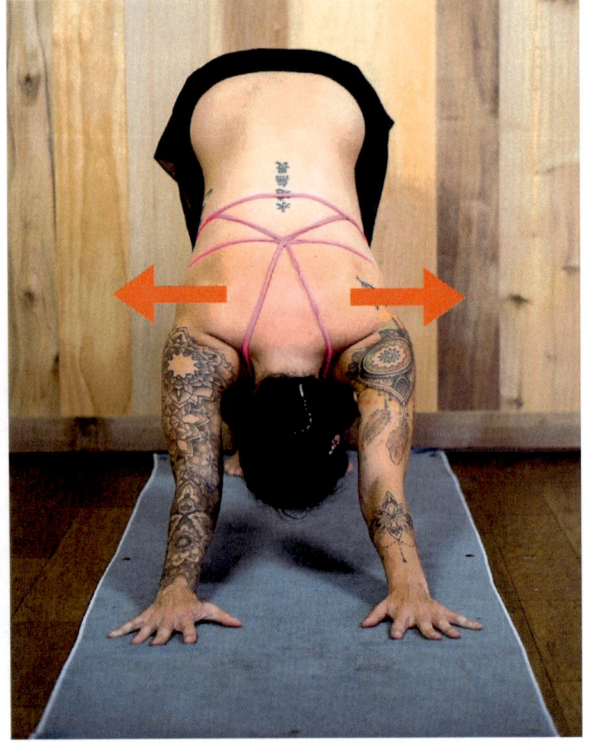

No Wrap (Incorrect)　　　　　　　　**Wrapped (Correct)**

Suggestion: Take 8-10 slow and controlled breaths here

Hollow Holds

Start lying on your back, arms by the ears and sides of big toe mounds touching

Inhale to engage the legs, pull belly button to spine, and lift the legs, head, and shoulders to hover off the ground. Do not lift either the feet or the head/shoulders more than 6 inches (goal is a slight hollow).

Note: It is all right to allow a small natural lumbar curve in the low back. Keep the navel pulled tightly toward the spine to protect the low back. Try your best to breathe normally.

To modify, simply keep the arms down by your sides instead of overhead.

Suggestion: 4 Sets of 5 breaths

Superman Holds

Start lying on your belly, arms by the ears and sides of big toe mounds touching.

Inhale to engage the legs, pull belly button to spine, and lift the legs, head, and shoulders to hover off the ground. Once again, do not lift either the feet or shoulders more than 6 inches

Note: You should feel both your abs and your back working here. Think slight lift, but also think extension through the fingers and toes.

To modify, simply keep the arms down by your sides instead of overhead.

Suggestion: 4 Sets of 5 breaths

Core Curl Ups

Start lying on the back, hands by your sides.

Lift the legs to 90°, pressing the sides of the big toe mounds together to activate inner thighs.

Interlace the hands behind the head, keeping the elbows wide. **(1)**

Inhale to activate your core and lift your tailbone off the floor by 1 inch. **(2)**

Exhale to lift the shoulder girdle off the ground by 1 inch, keeping the elbows wide. **(3)**

Inhale to lift both an inch higher and hug navel to the spine. **(4)**

Exhale release tailbone and shoulders back to the ground, but keep legs lifted at 90°.

Drill learned from Meghan Currie Yoga Teacher Training

Suggestion: 2 Sets of 10 core curls

Warrior III (Virabhadrasana III)

Warrior III is everyone's favorite pose, right?! Most of us view this very difficult posture as something to quickly struggle through and move on, but it's actually an amazing strengthener for handstand. Not only does it strengthen the entire body, it also sets up almost all of the alignment needed in handstand!

Start in mountain pose (Tadasana) with the feet together, sides of big toe mounds touching, hands by your sides.

Transfer weight to the right leg, but keep left straight.

Engage the core and hinge at the hips to fold forward with a flat back while the left leg raises up behind, foot flexed, forming a (T) with the body and moving like a lever.

Square the hips by scissoring inner thighs together and making sure that the left toes point toward the ground. This will also help level the hips by dropping the left sit bone (which tends to lift). Reaffirm core engagement.

To increase difficulty, put the arms by the ears, pinky fingers spiraled inwards.

Suggestion: 2 sets of 4 breaths per side.

Warrior III Handstand Levers

Holding Warrior III can be an excellent exercise, but finding some controlled movement while maintaining alignment can also be a key addition to your handstand practice.

These levers are a true test of balance, body awareness, and core strength, so don't be discouraged if they feel difficult when you first start practicing them, or even later down the line.

Start in a full expression of Warrior III with arms next to the ears (see previous exercise for cues).

Continue the lever movement as you further hinge at the hips to bring the torso and arms down to or towards the floor while the back leg lifts up as counter balance.

Continue to square hips and keep back toes pointed down with heel pointing toward the ceiling.

Lightly touch the fingertips to the ground, and moving as one controlled unit, rise back up to a standard Warrior III lever.

1   2   3

Suggestion: 5 times per leg, moving slowly and with control

The Art of Falling

There are a few things to get out of the way when discussing falling. The first was already discussed but bears repeating. When learning free-standing handstands, YOU WILL FALL. There's no way around it and you can do 10,000 drills at the wall, but once you start practicing L Kick Ups and other drills in the middle of the room, there will be many times that you need to "bail out" of a handstand. That's to be expected, and is something that you CAN and will get over in time. Like anything else, it just takes practice.

"....Is she really saying she wants us to practice falling..???"

Yeah. That's exactly what I'm saying. A planned fall is less scary than a sudden one, right? And if you get a certain movement pattern in your head, when you actually need to use it to "fall," it will feel familiar, and it is much more likely that your body will remember what to do. So I fully encourage you to practice the pirouette/cartwheel fall described herein, and to try it on both sides and maybe even when you're against the wall. Just to show yourself that you can do it, that it doesn't hurt, and that is can actually be simple, fun, and key to developing confidence with your handstands.

What Not To Do

In my opinion, everyone falls a little differently. You need to find the exact movements that work for you and your body, and something that will still be safe for your shoulders and wrists after say…5000 times.

As you probably expected, there are a few key things that you should NOT do when falling. This goes back to the myth about handstands being unsafe, but luckily, these can all be easily avoided.

If you're falling, DO NOT…Bend your arms

Your arms are holding you up. If you've been doing the drills and exercises in this book, they are likely strong enough to hold you up while you exit safely. The main goal of quickly exiting any pose safely is to protect the neck and back. If you bend your arms, you risk collapsing on the head/neck. So unless you have a great deal of gymnastics training and were taught to safely exit handstand with a forward roll (tucked neck), please avoid ever bending both arms when learning to handstand. Your body will thank you for it.

If you're falling, DO NOT…Let your body get loose

You're falling, but it's going to be ok. You've practice this, and you know what to do. In the moment of terror (because there likely will be some) do not lose your cool and allow your limbs to become wet noodles. The more controlled you keep your body, and the more core engagement you have, the more controlled your descent will be. Keep the legs engaged and navel pulled in to spine during the pirouette/cartwheel fall (described later).

If you're falling, DO NOT…Do nothing at all

What would happen if you did nothing at all during a fall? You've kicked up and your hips are past your shoulders, so you topple over. You may think you've got it all down by staying nice and stiff with an engaged core, but if you just do that, you're essentially doing nothing, and you will fall over landing flat on your back.

Yikes. Let's avoid that. If you're someone who tends to freeze up in new or scary situations, this might be something for you to consider, and maybe before you start working on free-standing drills, you take some time to simply practice falling. It will always be scarier the first time it happens accidentally, but being prepared can really help.

The Pirouette/Cartwheel (My favorite fall)

First, let's discuss a few different types of falls or "bail outs." The first issue might be that you didn't quite make it to vertical. Perhaps you didn't kick up hard enough to stack the hips over your shoulders and you're falling back the way you came. How do you safely exit this handstand?

The answer may seem obvious, but you would be surprised by how many times I've been asked that question. The answer is that you simply come back down the way you went up. Splitting the legs or keeping them in an L shape and making sure the arms stay straight with both hands pressing into the floor.

A much more likely (and scarier) scenario is that you've kick up just a little too hard or maybe a little crooked. Your hips are now past your shoulders, and if you were to do nothing, you'd probably fall flat on your back. But you're not going to do that. Because we just talked about how that was not a good plan.

Instead, you neatly pirouette/cartwheel out of the handstand and land on your feet. The pirouette looks a lot like a short cartwheel and involves pressing down firmly with one arm while allowing the other to become light.

The arm doesn't have to lift, just become lighter, and the body twists in the direction of the light arm. As you land, the legs bend slightly to absorb the shock. I suggest you try this carefully on both sides, and then select the side that feels more natural. For most of us, that means leaving our stronger arm down (my right), and lifting the other (my left).

So, if I was kicking up, hopping up, or pressing up, and accidentally gave myself too much speed, I would press down firmly with the right hand, allow the left to get lighter, and twist my body to the left to complete the cartwheel.

If you're falling slowly, this can be done slowly. The more that you "over kick", the faster you'll be falling, and the faster you'll need to make this pirouette/cartwheel. Which is why I recommend practicing it in a controlled fashion first so that it becomes a cemented body movement pattern that you don't have to think about; it simply happens when you're falling.

These pirouettes can also be practiced and/or executed as needed with the wall handstand drills, although they are likely to really only be needed with the chest to wall exercises that would allow your hips to pass over your shoulders and create the sensation of falling.

I recommend and personally use **the pirouette fall for EVERY handstand bail** that I do. In my experience, it is the safest method to quickly exit with the minimum amount of stress on the body.

(Pictures on the next page)

The Pirouette/Cartwheel (My favorite fall)

Hips come past shoulders

Left hand lightens

Body twists to the left

1

2

3

Continued Body Twist

Bend Knee to absorb shock

Hands lift with feet safely on floor

4

5

6

Falling to Wheel (Last Resort)

There are mixed views out there in the yoga world about "falling" into wheel pose (Urdhva Dhanurasana). Personally, I don't believe anyone should ever "fall" into wheel. It should be a calculated movement that is done with control from a scorpion bend position. If you're simply falling over quickly, there is no way you can do this in a controlled fashion.

But, there are some groups who are supportive of wheel falls, and I've had several fairly flexible friends who have told me that it's much easier for them to simply put a deep bend in the back and land in wheel. So for that reason, I just wanted to briefly address it in this book.

If you are someone who enjoys wheel pose and feels very comfortable in it, I would encourage you to warm up your shoulders, quads, and hip flexors before doing your handstands, so that if you did happen to over kick and bend in the back, at least your body would be more prepared for it. Care should be taken to land with as much control as possible, with the feet parallel (not turned out) so that there is less pressure on the low back.

Why Falling Into Wheel Is Not My Favorite

- It is typically a much faster and more uncontrolled fall.
- It takes more energy because then you need to exit wheel to get ready to try another handstand.
- Your feet are much more likely to slip out from under you if you don't get a deep enough bend, therefore causing you to splat on your back.
- This can be a very jarring exit unless you have exceptional back flexibility.
- Many of us inadvertently land with our feet turned out, causing extra pressure to end up in the lower or lumbar spine, the most common area for injury.
- It is much scarier than learning to pirouette/cartwheel out.

Single Leg

Double Leg

ALIGNMENT DETAILS

As with any yoga pose, we will start by building alignment for handstand from the ground up. Starting with the all important hands, traveling up the arms to the shoulders and back, stopping at the core/glutes, and finishing with the legs and toes, this section of the book aims to help you understand where each body part should be in space to help you achieve balance.

While it may seem like a great deal of information to process while you're also just trying to sustain yourself upside down, reading about the specific alignment and necessary activation can help you pick up bits and pieces, and you'll begin to see similar movements in other parts of your practice that you can capitalize on to help your handstand work. Slowly, these practices become body patterns that don't require quite as much thought, and over time, that can translate to better handstands.

Hand Positioning

When you flip your perspective in handstand, your hands become the "feet" that you stand on. It's not as simple as just throwing your hands down on the ground, but starting with a solid foundation will help to set your inversions up for success.

Setup

Traditionally, hands are set up shoulder distance apart for handstands. Since we all have different shoulder widths, this will differ from person to person. By holding your arms out straight in front of you, you should be able to accurately determine shoulder distance apart.

There are a few schools of thought when it comes to hands being placed parallel or turned just slightly out. Parallel hands mean that if you drew a line from the middle of your wrist crease out through the tips of your middle fingers, those lines would be facing exactly the same direction on both hands. Turning the hands out might be considering those lines and then turn each one out 20-40° from the midline.

Parallel hands are a more traditional teaching for yoga and gymnastics. They look neat, are simple to spot if not correct, and allow for easy balance of the four quadrants (described later). There is nothing wrong with parallel hands and you can achieve excellent handstands with them.

When I practice arm balances and inversions and even downward facing dog, I tend to turn my hands out approximately 25° from the midline. Hands that are turned out have a bit more wrist mobility (which is an issue for me) and also tend to put less pressure on the wrist over time. You get an added bonus of starting the proper external rotation of the arms necessary for handstand, (discussed later), which is always a great reminder for me to wrap my triceps back and the eyes of my elbows forward.

Finally, turning the hands out slightly forces me to root down through the index and thumb mound, which are the most likely to "get light" during inversions and arm balances, eventually leading to wrist irritation if not addressed.

I suggest you try both hand placements and see which works better for you and your practice.

Parallel    **Turned Out**

Four Quadrants

In many forms of yoga, you are taught about the four quadrants of the hands. These quadrants play into inner arch activation, even balance on all sides (which stabilizes the wrist) and can help set up the forearms and upper arms as well through small, but significant movements.

Quadrants: 1. Index Mound, 2. Thumb Mound, 3. Pinky Mound, 4. Outer Palm Mound

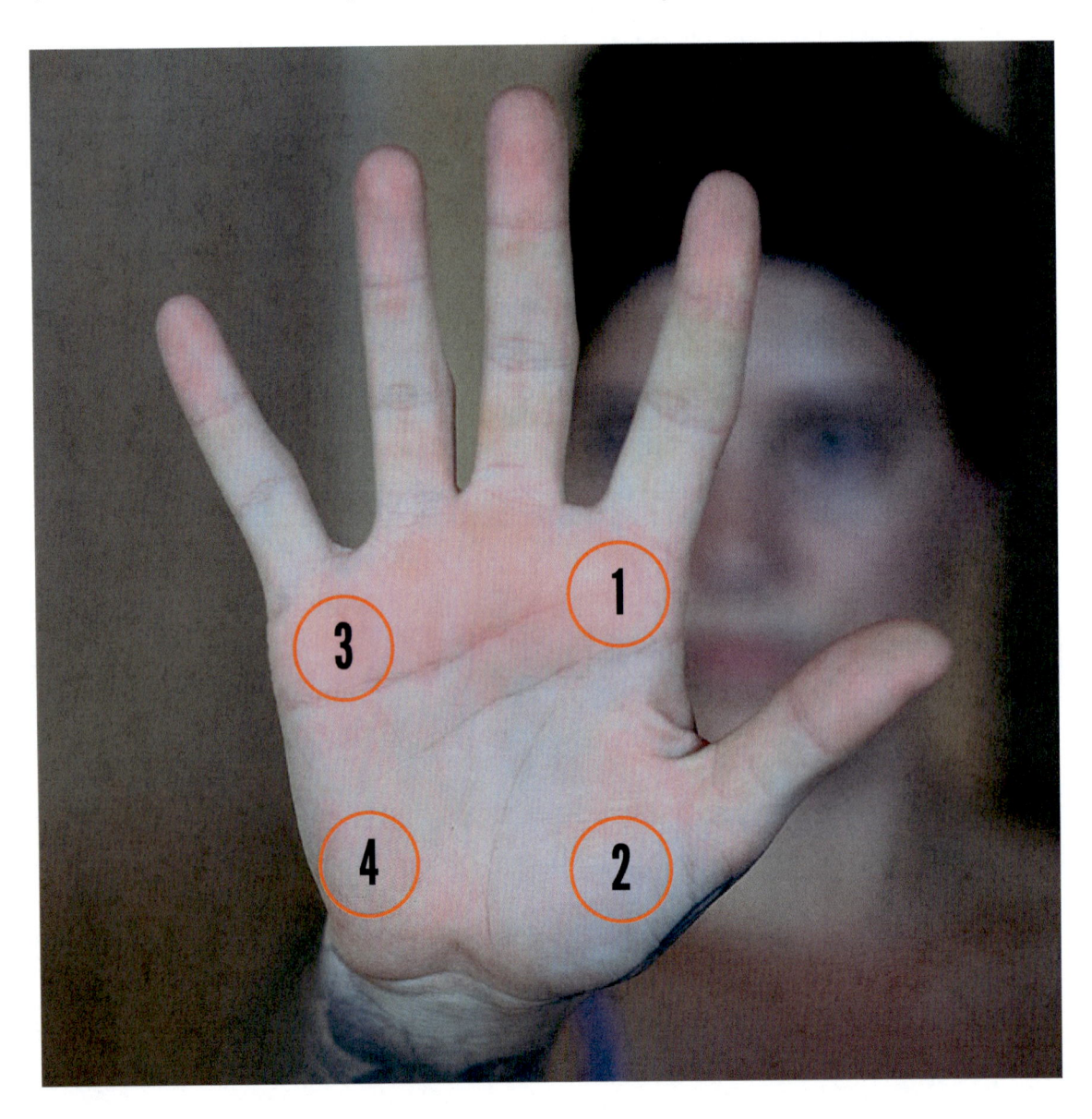

Four Quadrants

Four Quadrant Activation

- Practicing in table top, place hands on the floor, shoulder distance apart, either parallel or slightly turned out. Lift everything off the floor except the index finger mound. **(1)**
- Keeping everything except the index mound lifted, stretch down to the thumb mound and plant it firmly. Now very lightly, "smear" the thumb mounds away from each other like you were screwing on the lid of a jar. Your hands won't actually move; it's much more of an energetic or isometric motion, although you might feel your elbows get a little wide. **(2)**
- Keep those actions and stretch across from the thumb mound to the pink mound. Now magnetize those two mounds together – thumb and pinky. You may feel a lift near the center of the palm as the hand arches get activated. **(3)**
- Once again keeping those motions, stretch across to the outer edge of the palm, the only thing besides the fingers that still hasn't been activated. Root down through the outer palm mound, balancing out the outward "smear" that you did earlier, as you now imagine screwing jar lids on the other direction (outer palm mounds in), wrapping the triceps down again and turning the eyes of the elbows up. **(4)**
- Finally, fingers stretch out (not as wide as possible, just as far) and press down into the earth. **(5)**
- If done correctly, your hands should start to ache and get a really great workout. Hand activation practice can help to strengthen the inner arches and fingers, as well as work the forearms by balancing inner and outer spiral of the hands. All of which play an important part in handstand balancing.

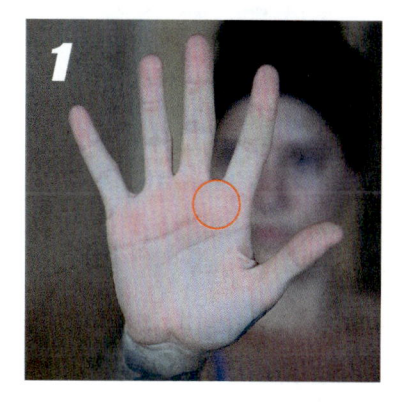

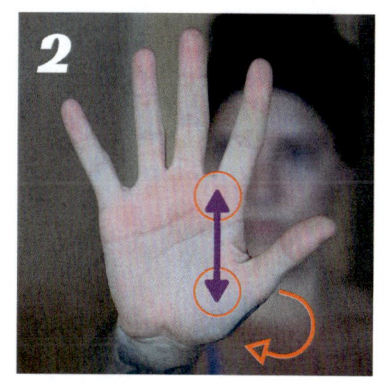

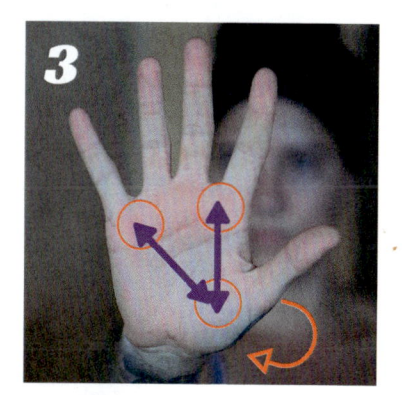

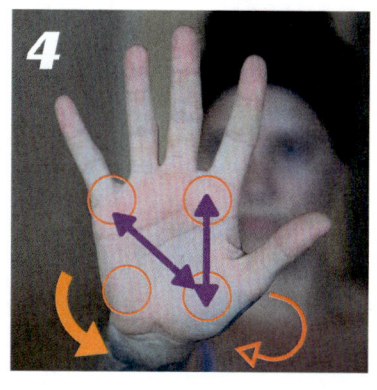

Where is the Weight?

The weight in a handstand is both everywhere and concentrated in certain areas. Sound complicated? It is. And it's always shifting a little because even when balancing in handstand, you are actually never perfectly still. Your fingers are doing all kinds of small movements, and you're moving the weight from one place to another in order to keep your balance.

Tips For Weight In Handstand

- Weight is along the perimeter of the hand with 60-70% in the inner hand (index and thumb mound) and 30-40% along the outer hand (pinky and outer palm mound).
- The centers of the palms are lifted, not flat on the ground. Think suction cup with the hand as the perimeter squeezes up toward the center to lift the arches.
- If there's one place that gets more weight than any other, it should be the index finger mound. This will allow you to easily access the palms for a little acceleration and the fingers for some braking.
- Fingers should be stretched long, but not spread out as much as possible. You need to be able to easily press them into the earth to calibrate.

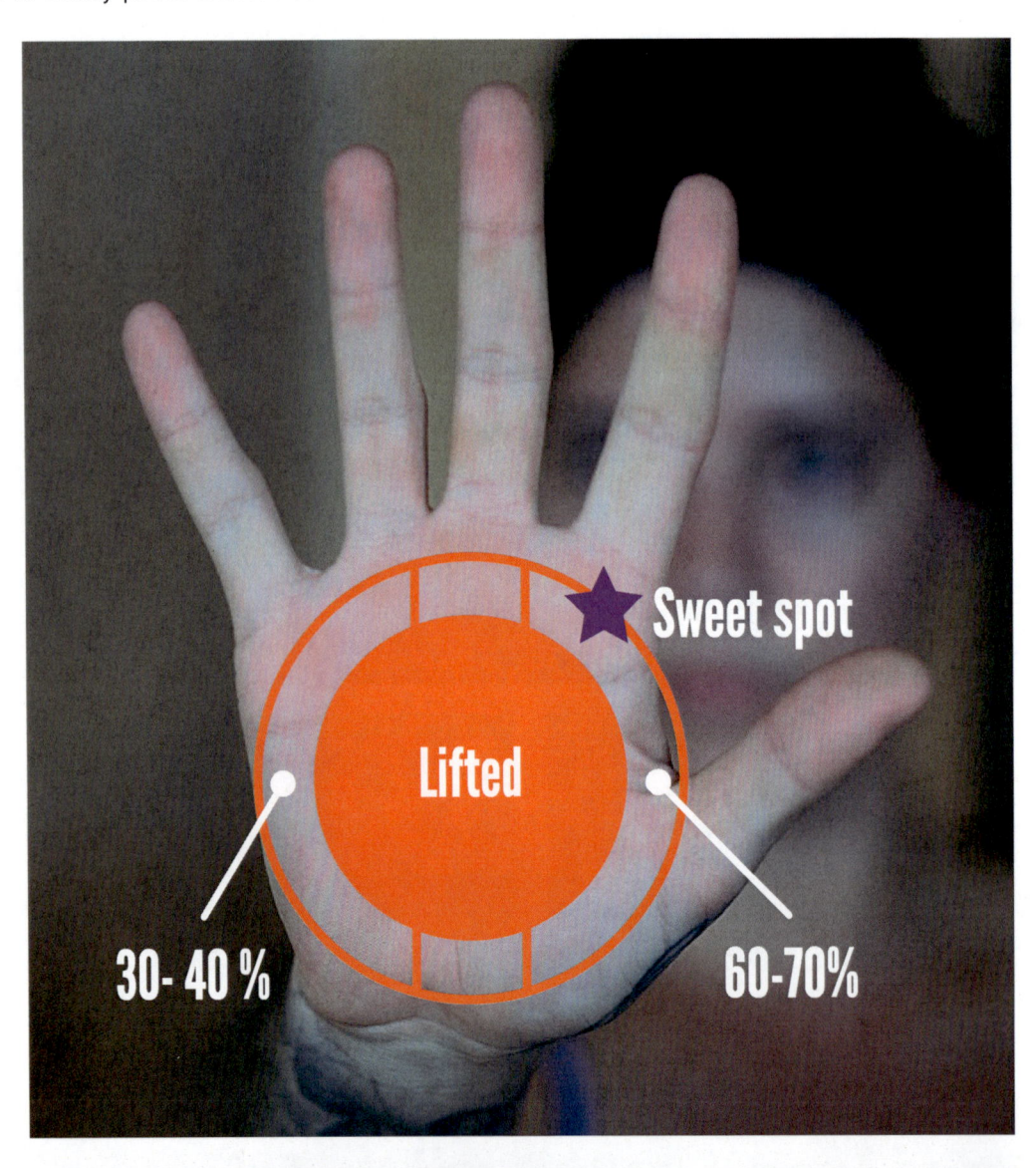

Arms & Shoulders

When balancing upside down, your hands essentially become your feet, your arms your legs, and your shoulders your hips. This is most problematic in the shoulder joint (actually 2 separate joints), as it is much more mobile than that of your hips. Mobility is great, but when piling weight on something mobile, you also need stability. So here are some tips and cues to help you find a little stability when hand balancing.

Tricep Wrap

Have you ever been in a yoga class and heard a teacher say to "wrap the triceps back?" It's becoming a more common cue these days, and is something that we practiced earlier in downward facing dog. You'll find that it's much harder to do while completely upside down, but it also doesn't have to be such a dramatic movement to stabilize and find broadness across the upper back.

A tricep wrap essentially means an external (outward) rotation of the upper arms. Your hands don't actually move, but the triceps wrap back around the body, while the eyes of the elbows start to face forward toward the finger tips.

You should feel a slight broadening across the upper back when this happens, as it causes your shoulder blades to protract, or move away from the midline. Tricep wrapping can also help with individuals who have hypermobile elbows (like me!) as it tends to limit the amount you can over-straighten the arms.

No Tricep Wrap (Incorrect)

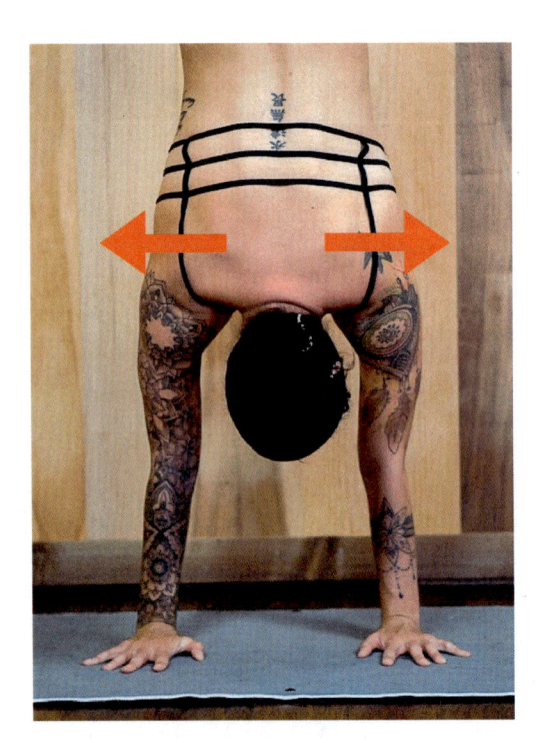

Tricep Wrap (Correct)

Neck Space

Another benefit of the tricep wrap is that "protraction" of the shoulder blades also brings them down the back slightly, closer to the sit bones. That means that even when you're pushing down firmly into the earth to lift yourself up, by doing the previously described wrap, and extending through the crown of the head, you should still feel like your neck has some length to it.

If your neck feels quite crunched up in your handstands, focus on lifting the shoulders away from the ears as you press up. Also, it is very common to lift the head too high (see next section on drishti), which will limit space in the neck.

Gaze

Gaze, or drishti, or focal point was one of the keys to handstands discussed at the beginning of this book. I can't stress enough the power of a strong gaze, as it can really make all the difference in balance and confidence on your hands.

Directional Tips

Gaze for handstands is typically suggested as "just past the fingertips." Please note that this doesn't mean you actually have to lift your head that much. You can gaze with your eyes without cranking the neck up.

The goal of handstand is to be fairly well stacked with wrists, shoulders, hips, and toes aligned. The more you bring your head out, the further the break in this line will be, and the more you start to change the position of your upper back. Bring the head out just slightly, and then look with your eyes in the middle and just past the tips of your fingers.

Changing Gaze

I do think there's something to be said for experimenting with gaze a bit to see how it affects your handstands. Having body awareness and understanding how small changes affect your balance is key to gaining confidence upside down. Using a wall, or a friend, try moving your head in and out a little, noticing how your center of balance shifts, and the changes you find in the shoulder girdle and upper back.

Once you start to feel comfortable with free standing balance, changing gaze can be a fun and challenging addition to your handstand practice. Many traditional gymnastic based practices focus on bringing the head down directly between the arms to complete the straight line, while others encourage an even further tucking of the chin to prepare for "hollowback" balances.

Regular   **Gaze Shift**

Picking a Focal Point

Although it may be obvious from the previous pages, do your best to select a specific focal point for your gaze. This tends to be true for almost any asana, whether it's for balance reasons or concentration.

Maybe that means starting with a small object on your mat like a penny or stone that you can place between your hands and just near the tips of your fingertips. Or just concentrating on one spot on the ground or your mat for the duration of the balance.

Starting your handstand practice in a quiet and private space can help you avoid distractions of gaze, and just assist with better focus in general. Of course, this works the opposite way as well. If you'd like to challenge your handstands, shifting your gaze or picking a moving focal point can be a great skill building tool.

Back & Core & Glutes

Back & Collarbones

The tricep wrap described earlier will externally rotate the arms and shoulders, to some degree pulling your shoulder blades laterally (away from the spine). You will feel a broadening in the back (just like in downward facing dog), however, you want to feel your upper back activated to balance out this wrap and keep the collarbones broad across the front of the upper body.

Practice engaging the upper back when doing the wall handstand drills, or have a friend lightly place a hand there when balancing to remind you to draw attention to this area and slightly "muscularize" the same area that you felt under the double block lay.

Core

The most common advice I give on handstand alignment has to do with the core. It is easy to forget about activating your middle when you're busy trying to stand on your hands and control your heavy legs. But keeping an active core is fundamental to holding a handstand in safe alignment.

The navel should be pulled close to the spine, fully activating the abdominal muscles. This movement will generally also bring the body into the tiniest hollow position, and knit the lower ribs in together, instead of letting them splay open with a slight arch…aka…the famous banana back.

Once I'm up in handstand, I'm constantly reminding myself to re-engage the core. As you start finding some balance or using the wall/partner for support, try running through a continuous internal scan of the body – fingers engaged, triceps wrapped, gaze steady, CORE engaged, legs active. Or have a partner near by tap you on the navel whenever they notice you could use a little extra engagement.

Banana Back   **Proper Form**

Glutes

To squeeze or not to squeeze? That is the question that has been circulating around the yoga world lately. It is my belief that activating your gluteal muscles (yes, I'm talking about your booty) is KEY to finding a lifted, strong handstand.

Your glutes are some of the biggest muscles in your body, and instead of the standard "tuck the tailbone" (similar to bringing the pubic bone closer to the sternum) cue, I'm much more prone to tell people to "muscularize and lift" the butt.

This creates a slight tailbone tuck anyway, protects the natural lumbar curve of the low back, and helps lift and secure the bottom half of your body skyward. You may also notice that squeezing your butt causes slight external rotation of the femur bones in the hip socket (because some of your gluteal muscles are external rotators), which we will discuss in further detail later.

It can be a little difficult to see the direct effects of squeezing and lifting the glutes in a free form handstand, but check out the wall drills section for an exercise that can help cement this engagement pattern.

Legs & Feet

Leg Engagement

I see a lot of fitness groups doing handstands or handstand walking these days. They are usually very strong and engaged in the upper body (and maybe even core), and loose as a noodle when it comes to the legs. That's not surprising.

We spend all of this brain power and concentration trying to firm our arms and shoulders to balance on that we forget we even have a lower half at all.

But your legs are a large portion of your body weight. Regardless of what leg position you use (discussed later), keeping them very active and engaged will be the only way to find true control in handstand. Remember the strong, straight legs you had in the Warrior III level drill?

Now is the time to find them again. Quads and calves working to help you move as a strong, calculated machine, not a floppy wet noodle.

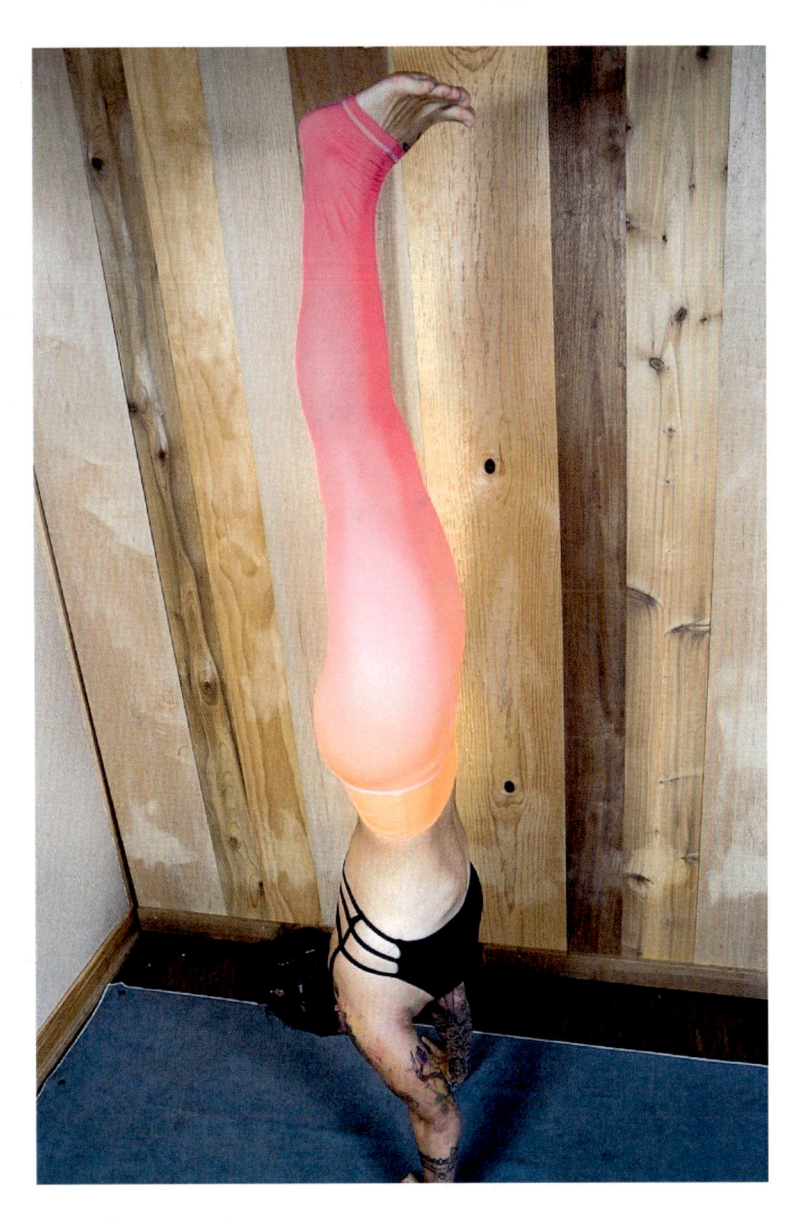

Feet & Ankles

Even the engagement of your feet can really help your handstand. Press the inner edges of the big toe mounds together, just like we did in the Core Curl Ups to activate the inner thighs.

Outer ankle bones work toward the midline, meaning they move IN slightly, causing a slight internal rotation of the legs to balance the external rotation from squeezing the glutes.

You may also feel the outer shins magnetize to the midline with the movement of your outer ankles.

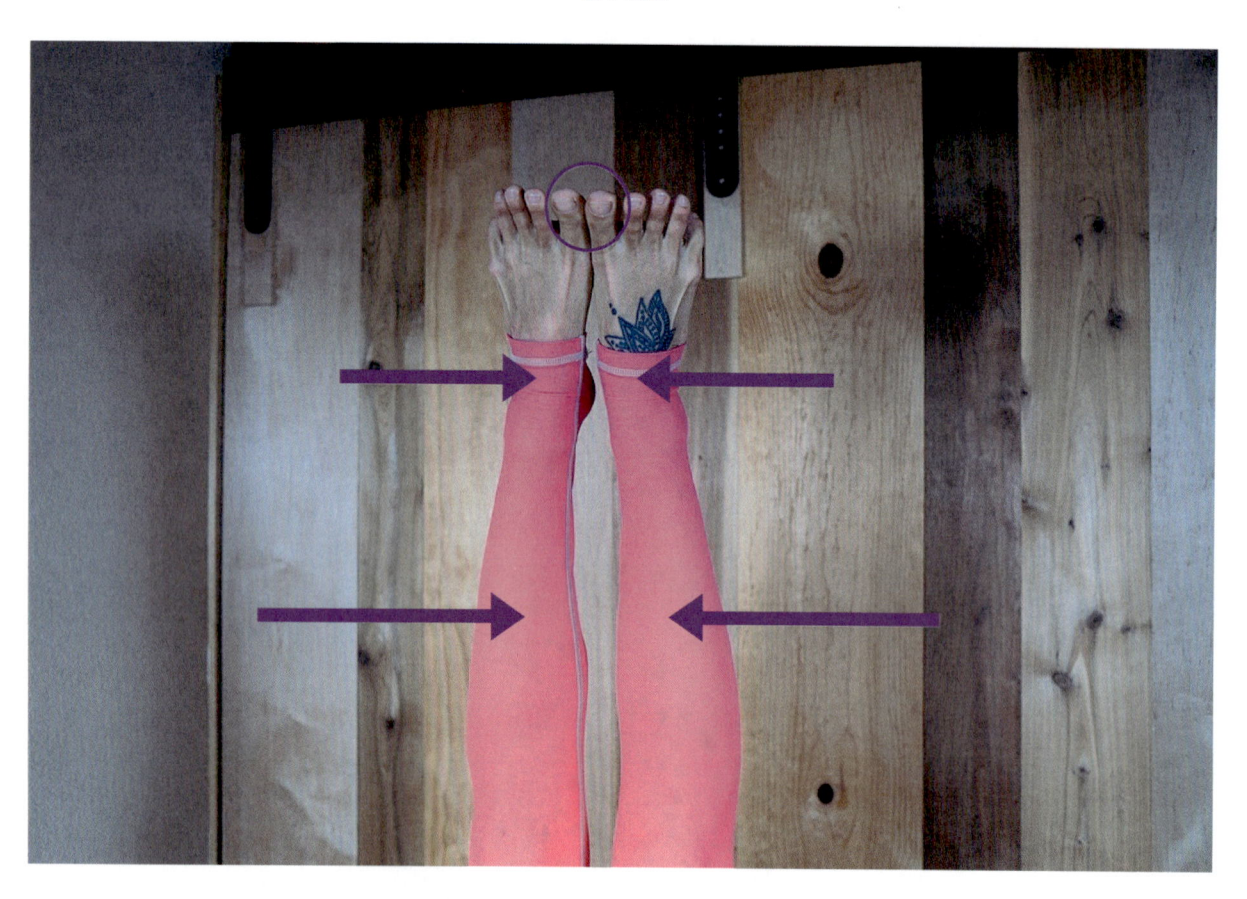

Point v Floint v Flex

Reading about the legs and ankles may have left you wondering what to do with the feet. Point? Flex? The in-between motion with long feet but active toes known as the "Floint?"

I've found that this is more of a personal preference, however, you should definitely activate your feet fully, regardless of whether they are pointing or not.

When first learning handstand, flexing (pointing the heel to the ceiling with flat feet) can be helpful. This really aid in creating a straight line from the palms up through the heels. If you consider the same extension through the heels that you did in plank, you may be able to find more lift.

Point    **Floint**    **Flex**

General Alignment

Got all that? There are so many alignment intricacies in a straight handstand. I hope that this section gives you a general idea of each by body part, as well as reference drills to work on these actions when you're not also trying to balance on your hands.

Try focusing on **2-3 cues at a time** (so as not to overwhelm yourself), and these movements will slowly become patterns that are easily incorporated into your inversions so that you can focus on other aspects.

If nothing else, consider the handstand a straight stack from the bottom of the palms out through the heels, with the entire body in full engagement, and only the head breaking the straight line with a slight tilt toward the fingertips.

Wall Assisted Drills

L Hold

- Properly measure distance from the wall by sitting in dandasana with heels against the wall and hands next to hips. **(1)**
- Place hands shoulder distance apart where sit bones were resting and come into a short downward facing dog variation with the back of the heels against the wall. **(2)**
- Adjust gaze just past the fingertips and take foot to the wall at approximately the same height of the hips in downward facing dog. **(3)**
- Press firmly to straighten that leg, lifting the hips up to stack over the shoulders, shoulders over the wrists, and swinging the other leg strong and straight up to form an "L" shape. **(4-5)**
- Re-affirm alignment cues with the first foot still on the wall. Run through the body from the ground up, focusing on engagement and alignment of wrists/shoulders/hips, and the top heel.
- Work the hold for 10-30 seconds and descend the same way you went up. Repeat with the other leg.

Float (Advanced)

Once comfortable with the standard L Hold, you may lift up and muscularize even more fully, leaning more and more weight into the hands until the bottom foot floats an inch away from the wall. **(6)**

Do not lift the second foot up to straight handstand when beginning this practice. Simply let it hover an inch from the wall.

Pike Hold

- Set up in the same way as the L Hold, with hands placed shoulder distance apart, the same distance from the wall as the sit bones.
- From the downward facing dog with the back of the heels on the wall, gaze just past the fingertips and step one foot onto the wall at approximately the same height as the hips.
- Firm and press into the leg on the wall, lifting the hips to stack over the shoulders, shoulders over wrists, and allowing the bottom foot to become light.
- Instead of swinging the bottom foot to the sky, place it on the wall next to the first, forming a pike hold or right angle with the body.
- Hold for 10-45 seconds, focusing on keeping the legs fully activated, and navel pulled deeply toward the spine (tendency in pike holds can be to arch the lower back instead of lifting up tall).
- Once comfortable, try the same float with both feet at the same time, hovering an inch from the wall as a great and very challenging core strengthener.

Modified Pike Hold

If the previously referenced pike hold feels like you're going to topple over forward, you can start with the hands further from the wall and still get a great core workout.

In fact, the farther from the wall you place your hands, the more similar the exercise will be to a lofted plank, and the more core work will be required to keep the body lifted.

Be sure to keep the navel pulled tightly to the spine to protect the low back when doing modified pike hold, and activate legs, firmly pressing the feet into the wall.

Note: You should not attempt the double leg float until you've walked your hands back so that the hips stack over the shoulders.

Chest to Wall

Flipping yourself around and utilizing chest to wall can be a great way to find proper stacking alignment and possibly experience your first "float." Be warned that getting into this posture can be a little awkward, but the benefits are boundless for your handstand practice.

- Place the hands shoulder distance apart, approximately 12-18 inches from the wall (simply to allow space to get up) and gaze just past the fingertips.
- Step one foot on the wall, as high as possible and press into it firmly to find lightness in the other foot
- Slowly straighten both legs up the wall, and carefully walk the hands in until the wrists are close to, if not touching the wall. (You can have someone spot you during this walk back to the wall to keep you from falling over).

Note: You may need to point or floint your feet for this drill, depending on how close you can get the rest of your body to the wall.

- With the front of the body flush against the wall and the gaze just past the fingertips, you should feel a proper stacking of the wrists/shoulders/hips/heels. As you fully engage the core, legs, and glutes to lift taller, you may feel yourself move slightly away from the wall and up, finding a moment of "floating" on the hands.
- Should you float too much and start to fall forward, remember the cartwheel/pirouette fall you practiced from earlier.
- Chest to wall holds can be done for 10-45 seconds, or as long as you can maintain good alignment and still exit safely. Exit by walking the hands out enough to allow you to descend the way you came up or using it as an excuse to practice the pirouette.

Wall L Kick Ups

Kicking or jumping up to the wall in a controlled manner is a great way to start practicing for free-standing drills of the same nature. When starting handstand, it is difficult to understand how much force is needed to get the hips right above the shoulders.

Not enough and you won't make it high enough; too much and you'll fall over and have to exit the handstand. With proper set up, the wall can help you translate the force needed to get there into your free-standing drills.

- Start with hands shoulder distance apart and 5-6 inches from the wall (just enough to allow space for the gaze just past the fingertips).
- Set up feet in a short downward facing dog, and lift one leg straight and strong behind, toes pointing to the ground, back of the heel to the sky.
- Keeping the gaze just past the fingertips and the arms straight and strong, deeply bend the supporting leg, bringing the chest close to the thigh.
- Use the strength from the bent leg to spring the hips up and back to stack over the shoulders, shoulders over wrists. The lifted leg can come to rest against the wall, while the second spring leg extends straight out strong, forming the popular L shape.
- Practice this hop on both legs for a balanced body and see if you can kick up just hard enough to lightly tap the first leg and glutes against the wall before coming down or finding balance. Keeping the core very active can help with this control.

- To add in a little extra work, experiment with using the bottom leg as a weight to pull you off the wall.
- After an L Kick Up, keep the back heel at the wall. Note: That should be the only thing touching the wall. Keep the core strong so that the glutes stay off the wall.
- Continue to gaze just past the fingertips, and keeping the front leg straight and strong, begin to lower it toward the ground, increasing the split.
- As it gets low enough, the weight of the leg will begin to pull the back leg off the wall, and there will be a moment of "floating" that will give you the sensation of balancing in handstand.

Tuck Kick Ups

There is another free-standing handstand variation that has become very popular for individuals with tight hamstrings or those who have a fairly strong core and don't want to worry as much about what their legs are doing while they try to find balance on their hands.

Keeping the legs in a tight wide tuck position (think inverted malasana or yogi squat) can be a helpful drill to find balance upside down, and just like L Kick Ups, utilizing the wall aids in determining the force needed to stack hips over shoulders.

- Start with hands shoulder distance apart and 5-6 inches from the wall (just enough to allow space for the gaze just past the fingertips).
- Set up feet in a short downward facing dog, and come up on the balls of the feet.
- Keeping the gaze just past the fingertips and the arms straight and strong, deeply bend both legs, bringing the chest close to the thighs.
- Use the strength from the bent legs to spring the hips up and back to stack over the shoulders. Legs stay bent in a wide squat, pulled in tightly to the body with heels close to sit bones, inside edges of big toe mounds touching.
- Practice hopping up just hard enough to lightly tap the glutes against the wall before coming down or finding balance. Keeping the core very active can help with this control.

1

2

3

4

5

Lift & Hover

- Kick or hop up to the wall using the L Kick or Tuck Hop method previously described. Hands should be approximately 5 inches from the wall to allow space for the gaze to be right in front of the fingertips.
- Bring both legs up to a straight position, feet flexed, with a foot of space between the ankles. **(1)**
- Engage the legs fully and lengthen them toward the ceiling.
- Squeeze the glutes, finding further lift in the heels. **(2)**
- Maintaining this lift, bring the flexed feet together. **(3)**
- Firmly pull navel to spine and press the earth down with the hands to hover both heels off the wall at the same time. **(4)**

Note: Even if they don't come completely off the wall, experiencing a lightening of your heels on the wall will still activate the belly and give you the benefit of the drill.

Drill learned from Christina Sell continued study

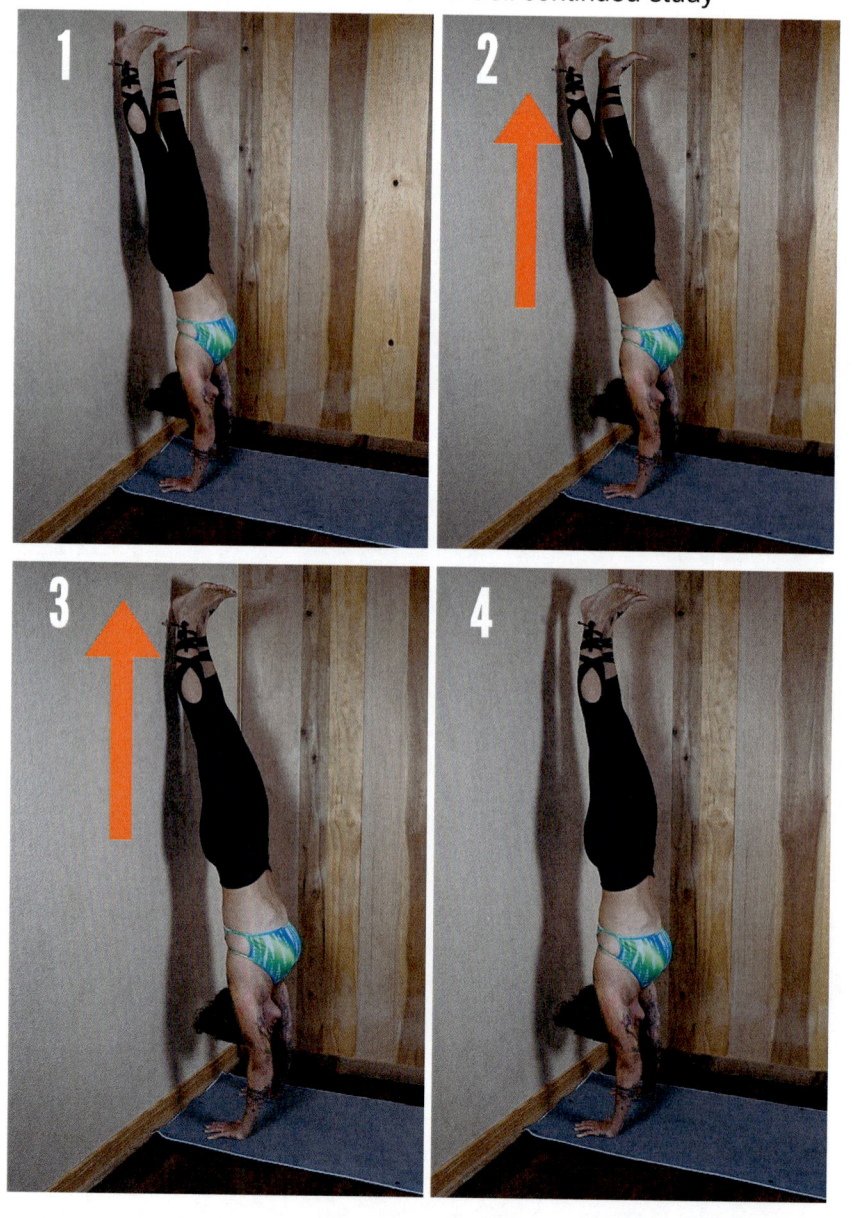

Double Wall Drill

Wall drills can help you find security in your handstands. They make it simple to determine the proper force for a kick up or hop up, and they help you focus on alignment since you don't have to worry as much about balance.

BUT...they can also help you practice the intricate finger movements needed to find and constantly recalibrate balance upside down. My favorite wall drill actually involves two walls or a doorway.

- Find a standard width door frame or an empty corner with two empty walls that you can work in.
- If utilizing a door frame, place hands shoulder distance in the center of the frame. If using a corner, place hands shoulder distance apart directly out from the corner, so that you're at a diagonal from both walls.
- Utilizing a modified version of the L Handstand step up, reach one leg up behind you to rest on the wall or door frame.
- Press firmly into this leg to the other leg past vertical so that both legs are straight and in a slightly split position.

Note: You may have to walk feet up or down the wall slightly until both legs are approximately the same height on either side of the wall/door frame. You're welcome to use a friend to help you find this position.

- Keeping the shoulders stacked over the wrists, gaze past the fingertips and firmly pull the navel to the spine
- Push the ground away with the palms and activate the legs to find additional lift.
- Hover one foot (front or back) off the wall and explore using the fingers and palms to gently shift the weight between the feet, perhaps finding a moment of balance between walls.

Note: To make this more challenging, lift legs slightly higher to decrease the split. You will no longer be able to keep both feet on the wall and will have to shift back and forth, aiming to find a moment of "hover" in the middle. Use the hands/fingers to shift your weight back and forth instead of just pushing off the wall with each leg.

Free Standing Drills

L Kickups

- Start in downward facing dog. **(1)**
- Step the right foot in approximately 1-2 feet to shorten the posture. **(2)**
- Lift the left leg up and back, straight and strong, keeping the hips square and toes pointing toward the ground. **(3)**
- Energetically pull the left femur (upper leg bone) up into the hip socket as if you were plugging it back into the body.
- Keeping the left leg lifted, inhale and come up on the ball of the right foot, shifting your gaze just past your fingertips.
- Exhale to bend the right leg deeply to load your spring, bringing the chest down toward the thigh. **(4)**
- At the bottom of the exhale, spring the hips up and forward using the power of the bent leg to stack them above the shoulders, shoulders above the wrists.
- Keep the legs straight and strong, but don't attempt to bring them together. Instead, hold an approximate L shape, which will be 90° or slightly more so. **(5)**
- Think of the back leg as your accelerator, while the front leg is your brake. Lowering the front leg will bring you back down the way you came, while extending the back leg past vertical will send your hips past the shoulders. Small movements of each leg can assist with balance and help you "float."
- Practice these hops 10-15 times on each leg, focusing on getting the hips over the shoulders, but not worrying if you don't make it all the way up there or find balance yet.

1

2

3

4

5

Tuck Hops

- Start in downward facing dog or a shortened downward facing dog (shorter dogs will be a little easier). **(1)**
- Inhale and come up on the balls of the feet, shifting the gaze just past the fingertips. **(2)**
- Exhale to bend the knees deeply to load your springs, bringing the chest down toward the thighs. **(3)**
- At the bottom of the exhale, spring the hips up and back keeping the legs tucked close to the body in a wide squat position (think malasana or yogi squat), inner big toe mounds pressing into each other. **(4-5)**
- Practice these hops 10-15, focusing on getting the hips over the shoulders, but not worrying if you don't make it all the way up there or find balance yet.

1

2

3

4

5

Moving to Straight Handstand

There is no rush to move the legs from an L Hold or Tight Tuck position into a straight handstand. Holding one of the alternative leg variations is still holding a handstand, and you will get all of the benefits of the inversion, as well as develop the proper alignment patterns.

Once you are finding balance for five or more seconds in an L Hold or Tight Tuck, you can explore slowly moving your legs to a straight and stacked position. The key here is to move slower than you would expect. Introducing any movement, even a controlled one, into your handstand will force you to utilize your fingers and palms to re-calibrate balance on the way up.

Always have patience with yourself and your inversion practice. Balancing on your hands is difficult, but also achievable with consistency, commitment, and attention to detail. More than anything, remember to have fun!

1

2

3

4

5

Partner Drills

A Word About Working Together

Working with a partner can be very conducive to learning a free standing handstand. Not only are there fantastic drills that need additional assistance outside of a wall, but partners can provide motivation and constructive feedback about alignment that may lead you to better balancing.

The most important things to remember when doing partner work are trust and safety. If you are the supporting partner in any handstand drill, never hold on to both legs of the inverted yogi. This does not give them any easy way to exit the pose if they need to, outside of collapsing in the arms. Instead, hold just one leg so that they can always carefully bring the other to the floor. Above all, listen to your partner and never push them to do something they are uncomfortable with.

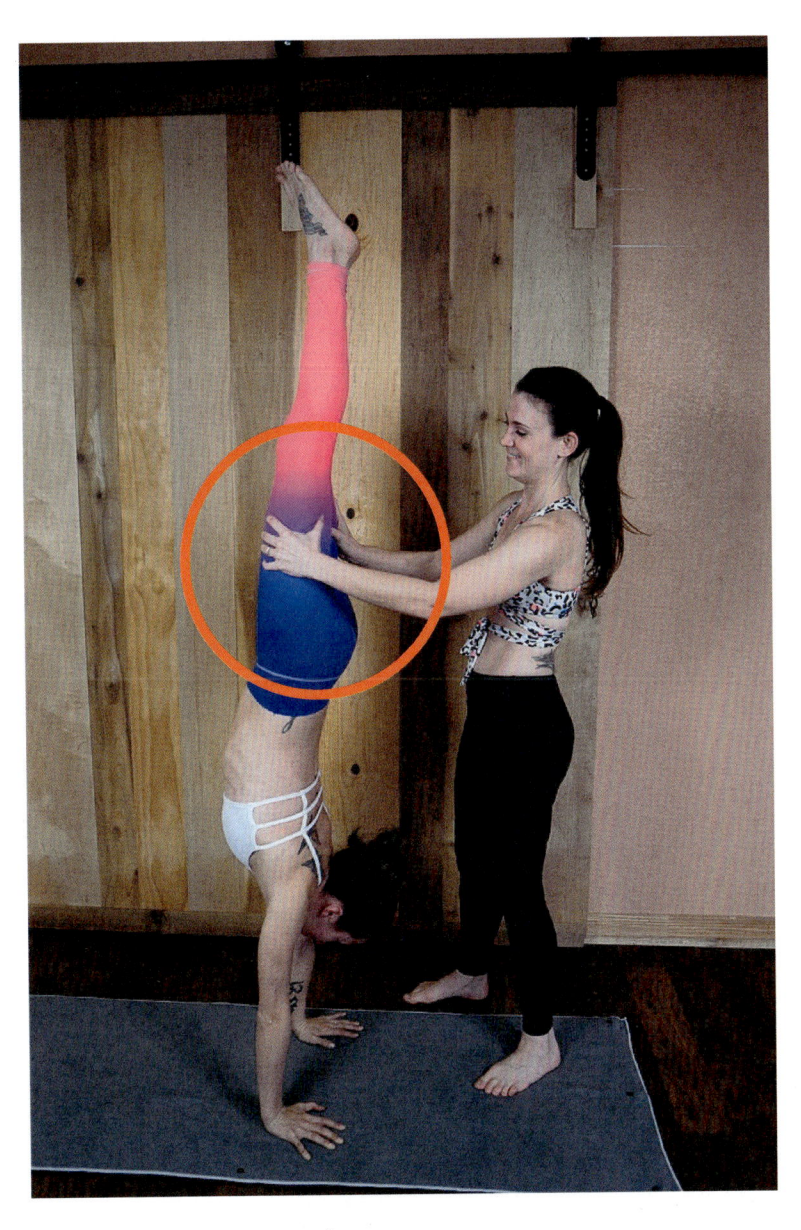

Incorrect

Downward Dog Shoulder Lift

Note: This drill can be practiced with hands 6-8 inches from the wall or in the middle of the room.

- Start in a downward facing dog with your partner standing behind and to the right of your feet.
- Shift the gaze just past the fingertips and lift the right leg straight and strong behind you, keeping the hips level and toes pointed to the ground.
- Your partner will grab hold of the right foot and gently lift it onto their left shoulder. **(1)**

Note: Supporting partner, use the left shoulder not the right so that you are not in the way of the ascent/descent.

- Using the shoulder of your partner as a shelf, lift the left leg up straight and strong to find an L hold position, pulling the hips up and back so that they stack over the shoulders, shoulders stack over wrists. Your partner will have to walk in carefully to allow hips to stack. **(2-3)**
- Hold for 3-4 breaths and then carefully come down.
- As always, make sure to practice both sides!

Core Killer – Heel Press

Note: This drill can be practiced with hands 6-8 inches from the wall or in the middle of the room.

- Start in a very short downward facing dog or forward fold with your partner standing behind and to the right of your feet.
- Shift the gaze just past the fingertips and lift the right leg straight and strong behind you, keeping the hips level and toes pointed to the ground. The goal is to get this leg parallel to the floor to make this drill accessible. **(1)**
- Your partner will bend their knees slightly and press their hand firmly into the right heel, applying pressure straight forward toward the hips. They can hold the ankle for added support.
- At the same time, you will press your right heel firmly into your partner's hand to find stability. **(2)**
- Using the pressure from the heel push as a wall, activate the core and lift the left leg up straight and strong to find an L hold position, pulling the hips up and back so that they stack over the shoulders. **(3)**

Note: Partner will have to walk in carefully to allow hips to stack.

- Hold for 3-4 breaths and then carefully come down
- As always, make sure to practice both sides!

Fist Assist

Once you have practiced a few straight handstand drills on the wall, utilizing a partner for freestanding drills can help you worry less about falling and focus more on alignment. This becomes especially important and helpful when dealing with straight handstands, as you no longer have the accelerator and brake of the legs, such as in L Handstand.

- Start in downward facing dog with your partner standing in front of and slightly to the side of your left arm.
- Proceed with the L Kick Up, lifting the left leg first and bending the right to spring your hips up and back.
- Your partner will catch the left leg firmly with their right hand, while the right leg is still parallel to the floor (forming the L shape).
- Once you have found steadiness with your partner's grasp, slowly bring the right leg up to meet the left, squeezing the inside edges of the big toe mounds together.
- Keeping a hold of the left leg with their right hand, your partner will make a fist with their left hand and place it between your inner thighs, half way between the knees and pubic bones.
- Once the hand position has been established, squeeze the fist with your inner thighs. Think about not just squeezing together, but also upward to find lift and length in your handstand. At this point, your partner should be able to let go with the right hand, therefore not really holding you, just allowing you to hold yourself on their fist, and exit any time you need to.

Heel Pressure Pose

- Start in downward facing dog with your partner standing in front of and slightly to the side of your left arm.
- Proceed with the L Kick Up, lifting the left leg first and bending the right to spring your hips up and back.
- Your partner will catch the left leg firmly with their right hand, while the right leg is still parallel to the floor (forming the L shape).
- Once you have found steadiness with your partner's grasp, slowly bring the right leg up to meet the left, squeezing the inside edges of the big toe mounds together and flexing the feet firmly.
- Keeping a hold of the left leg with their right hand, your partner will move their left hand to the top of your right heel. They will use their palm to apply pressure directly downward, encouraging you to push back against their palm and find additional lift in the handstand.
- Once stability has been found with one arm, the supporting partner can move the right hand away from the left calf and bring it to the top of the left heel, or simply continue pushing with one hand.
- With your partner's hand pressing down onto both of your heels, lift up through the shoulder, core, and glutes to press your heels up toward the sky.

Note: If using two hands, the supporting partner should not grip the heels, only push down with a flat open palm. This will allow the inverting yogi to exit the pose whenever he or she needs to simply by lowering one or both legs.

89

Hot Potato

- Start in downward facing dog with your partner standing in front of and slightly to the side of your left arm.
- Proceed with the L Kick Up, lifting the left leg first and bending the right to spring your hips up and back.
- Your partner will catch the left leg firmly with their right hand, while the right leg is still parallel to the floor (forming the L shape).
- Once you have found steadiness with your partner's grasp, slowly bring the right leg up to meet the left, squeezing the inside edges of the big toe mounds together.
- The supporting partner will slowly bring their other hand up close to your left leg.
- They will form an open cage around the leg allowing space for some movement back and forth, but with enough support to stop you from falling over or back down. Essentially, they will allow you, the inverting yogi, to play your own game of hot potato using their hands. Instead of pushing you off their hands, they will simply hold their hands firmly and allow you to use your core strength and finger balancing to pull the leg away from their hand and float once again. They are in essence, a much smaller version of the two sides of the doorway in the door frame drill.
- At any time, the inverting partner can exit simply by bringing one leg back down to the ground.

Do Create Cage   **DON'T GRAB BOTH LEGS**

Planks Drops (Full Body Strengthener)

- Start in plank pose, feet hip distance apart with your partner standing just behind your feet.
- Firm your legs and pull navel to spine.
- Your partner will squat down and pick up both of your feet from the ankles before standing back up and straightening their arms so that you are in a suspended plank. **(1)**
- After asking if you are ready, your partner will remind you to activate your core and then they will drop one leg from their hand. **(2-3)**
- Use your core strength to stop the descent of the leg and bring it back up to their hand.
- Proceed for 20-30 seconds, allowing your partner to surprise you with which leg they drop so that you are never anticipating the fall

Plank Pull Ups

- Start in plank pose, feet hip distance apart with your partner standing just behind your feet.
- Firm your legs and pull navel to spine.
- Your partner will squat down and pick up both of your feet from the ankles before standing back up and placing your ankles on either side of their waist, just above the hip bones. **(1)**
- Squeeze their waist firmly to activate the inner thighs. If you want an extra challenge, have them remove their hands from your ankles (since you are holding yourself there). **(2)**
- Continue to squeeze their waist and actively pull your hips up to stack over the shoulders, shoulders over wrists. Your partner will need to walk in carefully to allow you to do this. **(3-4)**
- Continue to squeeze their waist and lower your hips back down to plank, as they walk backwards. **(5-6)**

Note: The partner in plank uses the strength of their core and the grip of their inner thighs to pull the supporting partner forward and push them back. Never does the supporting partner just push the inverting partner's hips up.

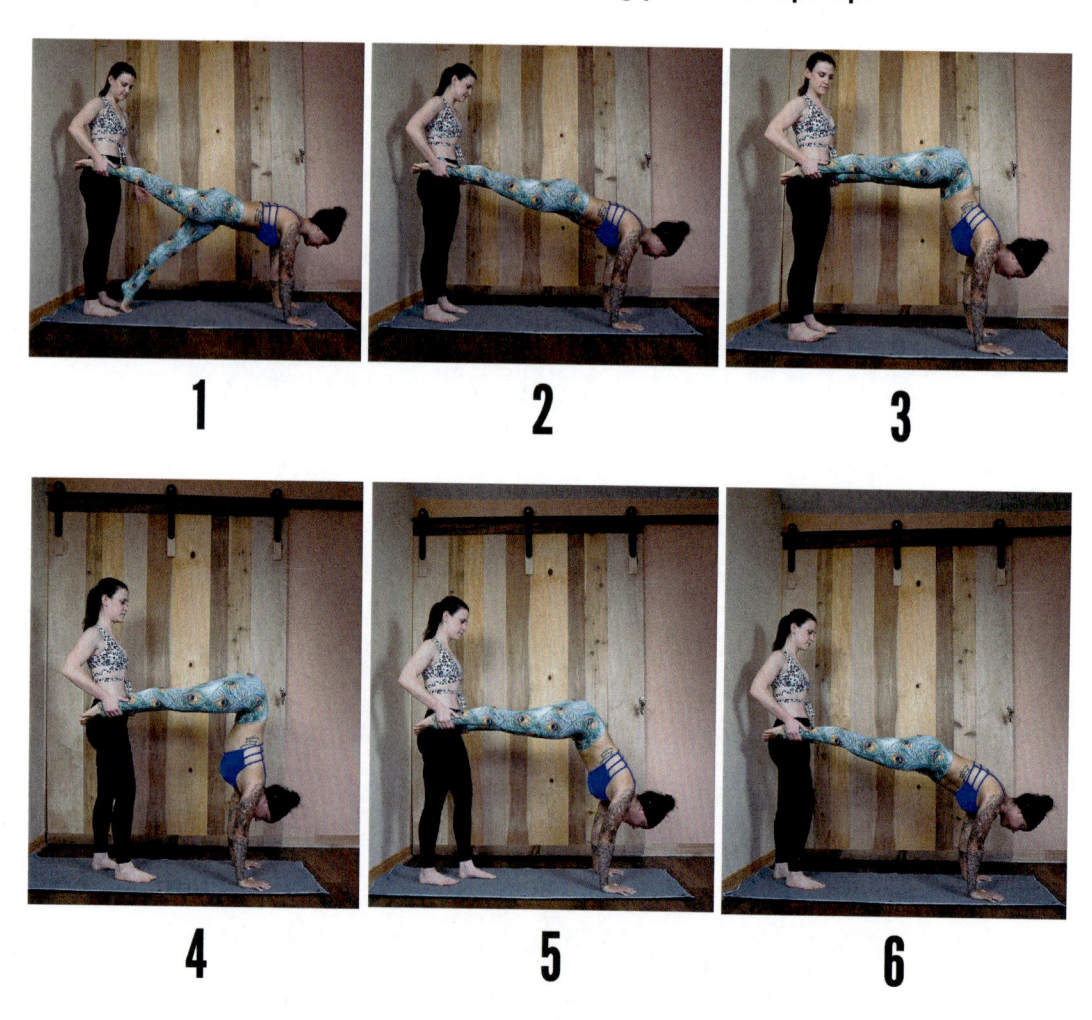

Suggestion: 2 Rounds of 3 Pull Ups

Restorative Poses

If you're dedicated to regular inversion practice, chances are you're working your body a great deal. Inversions take full body activation, which makes for a very strong core, shoulder girdle, and arms. But concentrating on muscularizing everything in straight body alignment can make you tight if you don't pair it with some restorative work in other movement patterns. This section will provide a few simple exercises that can help your body unwind after handstand practice.

Bridge – Supported

Supported (Block Needed):

- Start lying on the back, knees bent and feet planted parallel and hip distance apart with a block within reach.
- Reach the fingertips toward the heels to measure approximate distance feet should be from sit bones (having feet further from sit bones will lessen the bend).
- Inhale to press firmly through the feet and lift the hips up, raising the chest off the ground as well. Head, shoulders, and neck stay on the ground.
- Place block on the lower portion of the sacrum and near the tailbone. Placing it too high on the sacrum will increase the bend in the lower back when the point of the pose is to stretch the hip flexors. You may place the block itself at any of the three heights that you prefer to increase or lessen the lift.
- Slowly walk the shoulders under the body, drawing the shoulder blades medially (together) and down the back. If it is comfortable, clasp the hands together and press the back of the forearms into the ground to "puff" the chest up further.

Suggestion: Hold for 10-15 breaths, then remove the block and release

Standard (Setu Bandha Sarvangasana)

- Repeat supported bridge set up without the block under the sacrum/tailbone.
- Concentrate on lifting the hips and opening the heart up and behind the head.
- Keep the knees hip distance apart (tendency to splay out) and stretch from the knees to the back of the room to find length through the quads.

Suggestion: Repeat 2-3 times for 4-5 breaths each.

Chatush Padasana (Wrist Stretch)

- Start lying on the back, knees bent and feet planted parallel and hip distance apart.
- Reach hands back and grab outer ankles or low shins with thumbs pointing up.
- Inhale to lift the hips and chest up, slowly walking the shoulders underneath the back one by one.
- Keep grip around the ankles (or loop a strap around for grip) and pull the shins with the hands, while simultaneously moving the shins away from the hands to find a wrist stretch.

Suggestion: Repeat 2 times for 4-5 breaths

Prone Shoulder Stretch

- Start lying on the belly.
- Place right arm out to the side, forming a T, palm down on the floor.
- Tent left fingertips approximately 6 inches out from the left shoulder.
- Pressing into the left fingers, roll onto the right side of the body, bending the left leg slightly and allowing the left foot to rest gently behind the right knee (or on a block if it does not comfortably reach the floor).
- You should feel a deep stretch in the right shoulder. If you want less sensation, move the right arm in closer to the torso. For more sensation, bend the right arm at the elbow for a cactus shape.

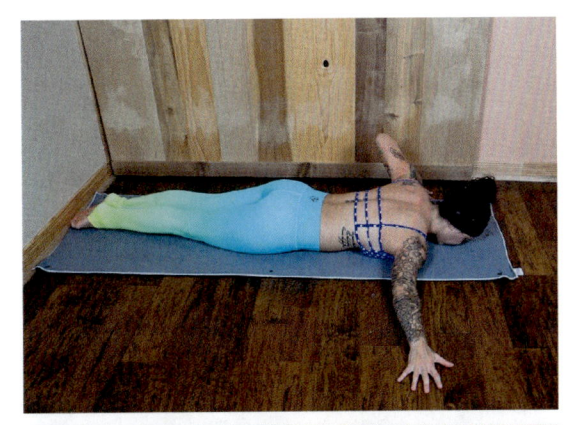

Suggestion: Hold for 10-15 breaths and repeat on left side

Reclined Hand to Big Toe Pose
(Supta Pada Gustasana)

(Strap Suggested)

- Start lying on the back, inside edges of big toe mounds touching and legs activated.
- Bend the right leg to bring the knee toward the chest
- Place the left hand on the left thigh and using the first and second fingers of the right hand, wrap them around the right big toe.
- Pull navel to spine to keep the core active and slowly begin to straighten the right leg, keeping the left leg on the floor with the toes pointing up toward the ceiling.
- If it is too difficult to easily hold the right big toe and straighten the leg, make a small loop in the strap and tighten it around the ball of the right foot, keeping the strap in the right hand.
- To any degree that you can, begin to pull the straightened right leg in toward the face, keeping both sit bones planted firmly on the ground, and the left thigh pressing toward the earth.

Suggestion: Hold for 6-8 breaths and then repeat with the left side

98

Spinal Twist - Double Knee

- Start lying on the back, hands stretched out to the side bent in a cactus shape, palms facing up.
- Bend the knees to 90° degrees and keeping them pressed together, lower both slowly to the left.
- Bend the left arm and press the left elbow and back of the head lightly into the ground to lift the torso up slightly and turn the left ribcage further to the right to deepen the twist and get the right shoulder closer to the ground. Pull navel to spine to create more space to twist.
- Release the back down to the ground and allow the left hand to rest on the outside of the right knee or place it back in catcus..
- Gaze over the right shoulder if comfortable.

Suggestion: Hold for 10-15 breaths and then switch sides

Spinal Twist - Single Knee

- Start lying on the back, hands stretched out to the side bent in a catcus shape, palms facing up.
- Bend the right knee to 90° and take the left hand to the outer edge of said knee.
- Use the left hand to slowly pull the right knee over to the left, twisting the body over the straight right leg.
- Bend the left arm and press the left elbow and back of the head lightly into the ground to lift the torso up slightly and turn the left ribcage further to the right to deepen the twist and get the left shoulder closer to the ground. Pull navel to spine to create more space to twist.
- Release the back down to the ground and allow the left hand to rest on the outside of the right knee.
- Gaze over the right shoulder if comfortable.

Suggestion: Hold for 10-15 breaths and then switch sides

Spinal Twist - Eagle Variation

- Start lying on the back, hands stretched out to the side bent in a cactus shape palms facing up.
- Bend the knees to 90° then cross the right leg over the left, double wrapping to hook the left toe around the left ankle if that is accessible.
- Press the feet into the ground and pick the hips up to move them 2-3 inches to the right.
- Lower the hips to the ground and then lower the wrapped knees to the left, allowing the body to twist.
- Bend the left arm and press the left elbow and back of the head lightly into the ground to lift the torso up slightly and turn the left ribcage further to the right to deepen the twist and get the right shoulder closer to the ground. Pull navel to spine to create more space to twist.
- Release the back down to the ground and allow the left hand to rest on the outside of the right knee.
- Gaze over the right shoulder if comfortable.

Suggestion: Hold for 10-15 breaths and then switch sides

Flows

Mini-Flow (I Only Have 10 Minutes)

2x 30 seconds of Kappata Bhati (1 minute) - Core	Table Top Wrist Stretches + Shakes (1 minute) - Wrists
Extended Puppy pose (30 seconds) - Shoulders/Upper Back	Plank Holds - 2 x 30 seconds (1 minute) – Full body
Down Dog (30 seconds) – Full body	Warrior 3 - 2 x 15 seconds per side (1 min) – Full body
3 minutes of handstand drills - at the wall, free standing, or both	2 minutes of spinal twists

Total = 10 minutes

HANDSTAND YOGA FLOW

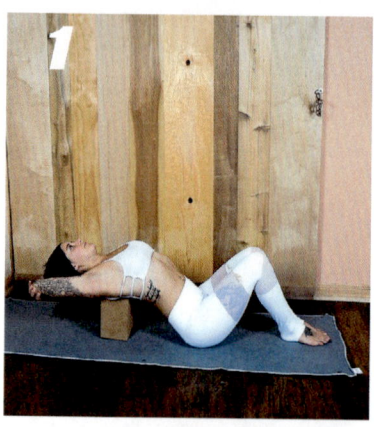

1 • Double Block Laying – 2 minutes
2 • Kapalabhati – 2 x 30 seconds
3 • Hero Twist – 10 breaths per side
4 • Hero Clocks – 10 breaths per side
5 • Forearm Wake Ups – 2 x 30 seconds
6 • Table Top Wrist Stretches & Shakes – 2 minutes
7 • Cat/Cow – 10-15 full fluctuations
8 • Sunbird – 10 full fluctuations per side (can be split to 2x5)

(Flow Continues on Next Page)

104

HANDSTAND YOGA FLOW (2)

9 • Downward Facing Dog – 5 breaths
10 • Roll to plank – Hold 30 seconds, rest in table top with wrist stretch. Then back to plank for 30 seconds.
11 • Lower through Chaturanga Dandasana
12 • Cobra – 2 x 3 breaths each
13 • (Roll to back) - Hollow Hold – 3 x 15 seconds
14 • Core Curl Ups – 2 sets of 8 full curls
15 • Boat Pose – 2 x 3 breaths (then rock to stand)

(Flow Continues on Next Page)

HANDSTAND YOGA FLOW (3)

16* • Warrior III – 3 breaths
17* • Standing Split – 3 breaths
18* • **Optional** L Kick Up – 3 attempts or holds
19* • Land in Warrior I, (cactus arms to find a slight back bend) – 5 breaths
20* • Pyramid Pose – 5 breaths
21* • High Lunge – 3 breaths
22* • Step back to Downward Facing Dog – 5 breaths
23* • **Optional** Hop to Tuck Hold – 3 attempts (landing in a short downward facing dog each time)
24* • Malasana – 5 breaths
25* • **Optional** Crow Pose – 1-2 minutes of play

(Flow Continues on Next Page)

106

HANDSTAND YOGA FLOW (4)

26* • Malasana – 5 breaths
27* • Forward Fold with Hand Release (shake it out) – 10 breaths

16 – 27 Stand and repeat left side

28 • Open Inversion Play (drills of your choice) - 5-10 minutes
29 • Child's pose – 10 breaths
30 • Roll to back followed by Bridge – 3 x 5 breaths
31 • Optional Chatush Padasana for the wrist release – 5 breaths
32 • Reclined Spinal Twist variation – 10 breaths per side
33 • Supta Padangustasana – 10 breaths per side
34 • Savasana (5-10 minutes)

107

CLOSING

Thank you to everyone for purchasing and taking the time to read my book. I am honored to share the drills, exercises, and key concepts that have helped me with my handstand practice and over all yoga growth. I hope that you find the content of this book useful for your personal yoga journey, and that if inversions are something you already are or find yourself passionate about, you continue the quest for additional knowledge on the subject.

It is my humble opinion that a book (electronic or not) is a wonderful tool, however, nothing can replace solid one on one time with an experienced practitioner. This is generally true to all forms of yoga, not just getting upside down on your hands. While the costs of private sessions these days can vary greatly, students typically benefit significantly from even 4-5 lessons that focus on alignment (specific to your body), and strengthening any areas that you or your teacher feel have opportunity. Even if your experiment with private sessions is a short one, you can still take the information gleaned back to your personal practice or into public flow classes.

If you're interested in learning more about handstands, there are an abundance of resources available. From handstand specific flow bundles through programs such as CodyApp to local workshops or traveling teacher visits, there are likely to be a variety of resources, and you can pick the one best suited to your needs. If you're not sure where to start, call up a local studio. Ask if they have or know of any workshops coming to the area, or perhaps have a teacher who specializes in teaching inversions. As inversions grow in popularity, more and more "flight" classes are being added to studio repertoires.

Above all, have patience with yourself and your practice. The inversion journey can be very different for each of us. Regardless of how long it takes you to stand confidently on your hands, regular consistent practice is the key to getting there. So don't dismay if you aren't the king or queen of handstands by the end of week one. Cut your beautiful body, heart, and mind a little slack and keep at it. The journey is half the fun anyway. Probably even more so.

ACKNOWLEDGEMENTS

There are so many people I would like to thank for helping me make this book possible.

Rabah Rahil for his creative genius in photography and graphic design.

Erin Kelly, Holly Fiske, Natasha Swinford, and **Toni Bopp** for their time spent editing – both grammar and content.

My amazing husband, **Ben House**, for putting up with my constant handstand antics, my requests for "just one more handstand picture" and his patience with the countless hours spent pouring over my computer to try to get this book organized.

Sydney Ring and Keely Rizzato for their assistance in the Partner Drill section, and their help with alignment during the longest photoshoot ever.

Meghan Currie, for starting my journey as a yoga teacher with her 200 HR training.

Christina Sell and Gioconda Parker for continuing my journey with their 300 HR training.

Carson Calhoun, Patrick Beach, Kim Schaefer, Tiffany Cruikshank, and many other amazing local teachers for the workshops that I attended on inversions that helped add to this drill repertoire.

And finally, every single one of you – for motivating me to continue my own handstand practice, for asking important questions when it comes to inversions, and for believing in me enough to share some of our journey together by purchasing this book.

Thank you.

COMING SOON

The Beginner's Guide to Handstand Pressing

The Beginner's Guide to Arm Balances

The Beginner's Guide to Lotus

The Beginner's Guide to Forearm Stand

The Beginner's Guide to Headstand

The Beginner's Guide to Backbends

The Beginner's Guide to Splits

And More...

SNEAK PEEK AT THE BEGINNER'S GUIDE TO PRESSING

01. Mat Walks

02. Puppy Press

Mat Walks

- Start at the back of the mat, feet mat width apart and parallel.
- Hinging at the hips, fold forward with a flat back, bringing the hands down, shoulder distance apart with the back of the wrists approximately 3-4 inches in front of the toes.
- Rise up onto the balls of the feet, shifting more weight into the hands.
- Press the earth down firmly to feel the shoulders lift up and allow the back to round slightly as the shoulder blades protract (move away from the midline).
- The back should begin to resemble the "cat" position from cat/cow.
- Pull the navel firmly to the spine, lift the quads to activate the entire leg and leaning further into the hands, feel the toes get light until you can lift both feet off the ground at the same time and float them 3-4 inches forward, closer to the hands.
- Move hands 3-4 inches forward and repeat the process.

Note: These may not look like a "float" at the beginning. Even the preparatory stages of this drill (i.e. just setting up and protracting the shoulders) will give you the benefits of the exercise. Do your best to avoiding hopping, as it is the transfer of weight to the arms, and the "plugging in" of the femur bones into the hip sockets that allow the body space to lift the legs and move them forward. Eventually, this drill can be done backwards or with legs together to increase difficulty.

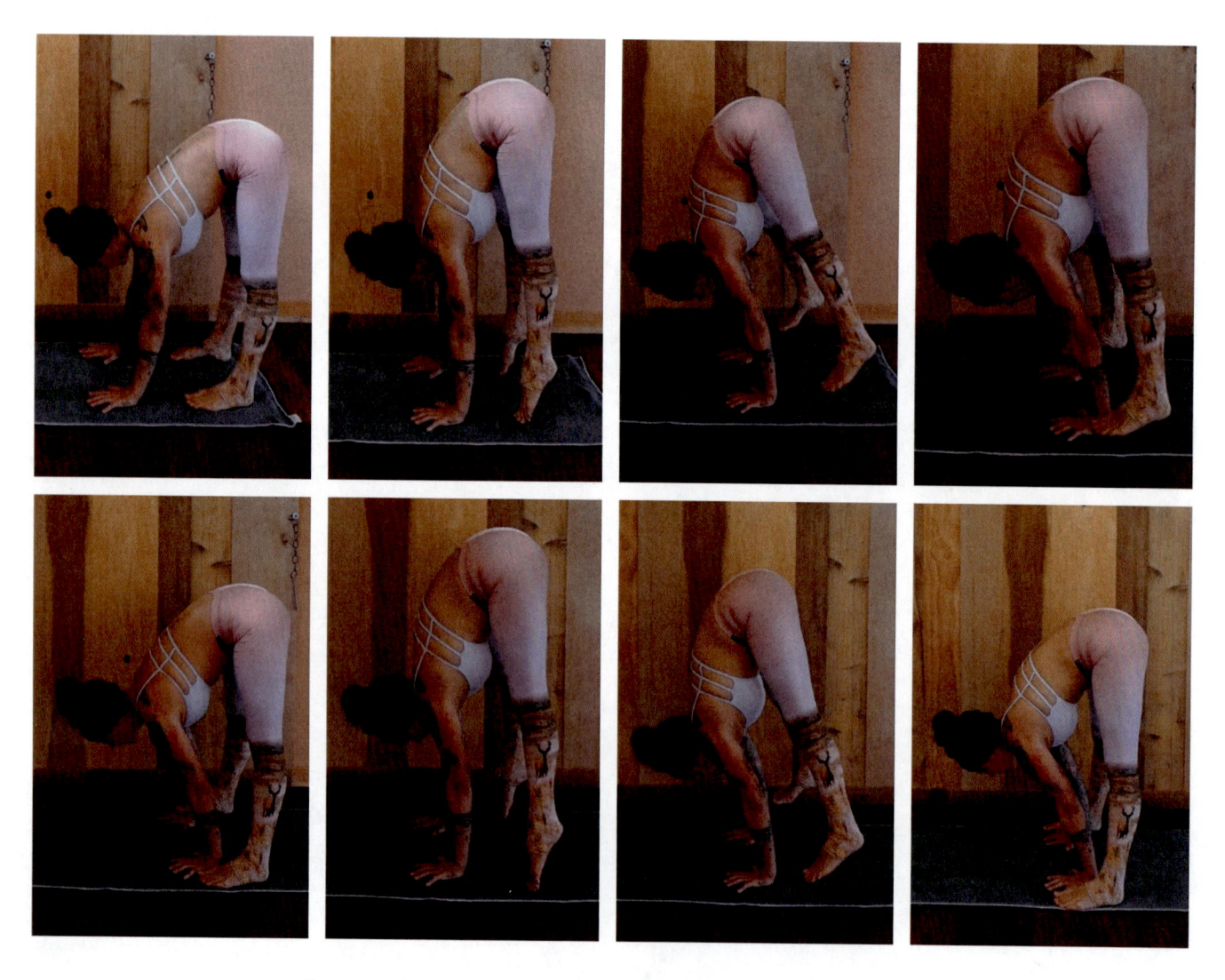

Suggestion: Travel the distance of the mat 3 times

The Puppy Press

The puppy press can be a step in learning the full body activation needed for handstand pressing. Essentially, a puppy press is a one legged press, with the lifted leg bent but held high to assist in stacking the hips above the shoulders. The bent leg is still active and engaged, but allows for the focus to be on lifting only one leg, instead of two. It is important to practice the puppy press on both sides to maintain balance in the body.

- Start at the back of the mat, feet mat width apart and parallel.
- Hinging at the hips, fold forward with a flat back, bringing the hands down, shoulder distance apart with the back of the wrists approximately 3-4 inches in front of the toes.
- Rise up onto the balls of the feet, shifting more weight into the hands.
- Prepare the right foot to support the body like a kick stand, and then lift the left leg, allowing the hip to open and the knee to bend, with the left foot reaching toward the sit bones and the left knee reaching up to the sky (think of the wild thing entrance from downward facing dog)
- Press the earth down firmly to feel the shoulders lift up and allow the back to round slightly as the shoulder blades protract (move away from the midline).
- The back should begin to resemble the "cat" position from cat/cow.
- Pull the navel firmly to the spine, lift the quads of the right leg and leaning further into the hands, feel the right toes get light.
- Once the toes are light, keep full body engagement and concentrate on pressing the right toes out to the sides (instead of up). Eventually, the right leg will lift and "float" up to a straddle hold, at which point, it can stay there or be brought to a straight handstand to complete the press.
- Modify by placing the right foot up on 1-2 blocks for additional height. The idea is to get the hips up as high as possible so that less work is required by the shoulders and core to lift the pelvis.

Alternative View Puppy Press

Made in the USA
Middletown, DE
11 May 2019